T0065308

ADDICTION
AND
GOD

Reconciling Science with the Spirit

MICHAEL K. MASON

WestBow
PRESS®
A DIVISION OF THOMAS NELSON
& ZONDERVAN

WestBow Press books may be ordered through booksellers or by contacting:

WestBow Press
A Division of Thomas Nelson & Zondervan
1663 Liberty Drive
Bloomington, IN 47403
www.westbowpress.com
1 (866) 928-1240

ISBN: 978-1-5127-0104-3 (sc)
ISBN: 978-1-5127-0106-7 (hc)
ISBN: 978-1-5127-0105-0 (e)

Library of Congress Control Number: 2015920540

Print information available on the last page.

WestBow Press rev. date: 01/20/2016

CONTENTS

Part III - Addiction and the Holy Spirit

INTRODUCTION

I CAN HONESTLY SAY that I never really intended to write a book. I haven't written anything of consequence since I graduated from Syracuse University in 1991. Back then, I had to write a long thesis on the "Economics of the Great Depression" and I must admit it wasn't a whole lot of fun. In much the same way, the process of researching and compiling the data for this book was by no means a "walk in the park." Some of the studies and accompanying data are quite complicated, so I have attempted to break down this information into more understandable terms. I'm not a physician or a scientist, and I assumed simplifying these topics would benefit the reader as much as it benefited me.

I'm not a trained addiction counselor or a psychiatric clinician, which actually worked in my favor in this exercise. Having seen the wreckage of addiction first-hand, I was curious (as a layperson) about addiction as a concept. My brother struggled mightily with drug abuse, and I had my own struggles as a young person with alcohol. I was influenced for years by the disease theory of addiction, and I wanted to understand the forces that drive this destructive behavior. Because I have no formal training in addiction science, I was able to attack the subject without the preconceptions that accompany the prevailing disease theory of addiction. I started by reading as much as possible on the subject, but not with the idea that I was researching a book. I was simply trying to satisfy my innate curiosity about the forces involved in triggering addictive behaviors.

I began this process with an open mind, not realizing that I was doing anything other than trying to learn. I am well aware of the defects in my own character, and my brother and I talked quite often about the differences between choice and compulsive behavior. However, the more

I read about the disease theory of addiction, the more confused I became. The fact that "addicts" are born different and have no control over their behavior made little sense to me. Growing up in a church environment, I was familiar with the concept of free will and its corresponding relationship with sin. I also knew that my brother never really began to control his addiction until he started to embrace spirituality and accept responsibility for his actions.

As I became more obsessed with solving the riddle of addiction, I began to volunteer my time counseling others in a well known program called Celebrate Recovery. This biblical recovery program is based on the 12 Steps to Sobriety promoted by Alcoholics Anonymous. I then started to develop a more complete understanding of the complex relationship between addiction and spirituality. After years as the local Director of a Celebrate Recovery program, I began speaking to churches and youth groups on the nature and repercussions of addiction. I enrolled in a pastoral training program shortly thereafter and am now a fully ordained minister.

Years ago, I began to volunteer my time as a mentor/counselor in the very successful Drug Court program in Lee County, MS. This allowed me to enlarge my circle of influence, as I came into contact with hundreds more people that were struggling with substance abuse. I'm thankful to Judge Ricky Thompson and the many great people I've worked with over the years in this program, as it helped me to expand my base of knowledge and real life experience on the front lines of the war against substance abuse.

The pages that follow are the culmination of these years of research and real life experience with addiction and its aftermath. The first section of this book deals exclusively with the science and suppositions that surround the divergent opinions of today's experts on addiction. It includes many statistics, quotes, and concepts that are attributed to some of the leading thinkers in the field. The results of my investigation may surprise you, but they are substantiated by some of the best and brightest minds in the study of addiction today.

The latter sections of this book deal with the religious implications of addictive behaviors. I am not a trained theologian, nor do I claim to be a gifted scholar of the bible. I have attempted to keep the spiritual discussions on a fairly simple level so that the principles intended will not be too hard to comprehend. All scripture is quoted with permission from the New International Version (NIV) of the Bible.

I wish to state clearly that I have no "ax to grind" with AA or the addiction recovery industry. There are many brilliant people who work hard in attempting to help substance abusers reclaim their lives, and I have the utmost respect for every one of them. Alcoholics Anonymous is a worthwhile organization that has helped many people over the years, and I wish not to offend anyone affiliated with it. I think we all have the same goal—to help people that are struggling.

I would never presume to judge another person by the quality of his/her behavior. My own personal history is filled with a variety of missteps and mistakes that I am willing to recognize and accept. I am in no position to judge or look down upon anyone. I am first and foremost a sinner—a fact I'm reminded of daily. In this context, I'm not attempting to judge you as an "addict"—rather I'm trying to get you to judge yourself. My hope is that by encouraging others to realize their own limitations, this book can help them secure a more intimate relationship with God.

As I said, I really never intended to write this book. But having learned what I've learned and seen what I've seen, I really had no choice. You'll find the story of my family's brush with addiction offered in small doses that are woven throughout the manuscript. This narrative is absolutely true and verifiable. These dramatic events have not been embellished—our family story is as real as living with addiction can get. When I look back on my life, I'm reminded of the words of my favorite writer, the Apostle Paul:

> *Now I want you to know, brothers and sisters, that what has happened to me has actually served to advance the gospel.*
> **—Philippians 1:12**

PART I

The History and Science of Addiction

"Addiction does not mean that God in heaven decided which people are alcoholics and addicts."

—Stanton Peele, Ph D
Author and Addiction Researcher

CHAPTER ONE

Addiction and Evel Knievel

A man can fall many times in life but he's never a failure if he tries to get up.

—Robert "Evel" Knievel

THE VIBRATION OF the motor cuts right through you like an electric knife through a Christmas ham. Adrenaline shoots through your body and mixes with an exhilarating twinge of fear until you can almost taste it. The anticipation may not kill you—but the foolhardy jump just might. The time for talk has ended. Do it or don't—it's time to make a choice. You abandon reason and fear by releasing the brake and hitting the throttle, building speed and courage as you go. You hit the bottom of the ramp with ferocious determination, gaining momentum as you accelerate toward the launch point. There's no turning back now.

You leave the ramp behind and soar skyward like a rocket with a built in soul. You reach the apex of your flight and are as "high" as you've been in your life. The view is spectacular, as is the euphoria of the moment. But as you look ahead, you begin to brace for the wreckage and ruin that is to come. You're losing altitude fast and headed for a painful, messy landing. Touchdown is rougher than you'd imagined, as you hit the ground hard and end up in a twisted heap of metal, bone, and flesh. When you finally slide to a bloody halt, you are fortunate to have survived the effort. You've thumbed your nose at God once again, and whistled your way past the graveyard. "When," you ask yourself, "can I do it again?"

Likewise, I can recall with clarity the time I wrecked my prized Evel Knievel bicycle as a kid while attempting a death-defying jump of my own. The flight was exhilarating, but the landing was not. I flew head first over the handlebars and skidded to a stop on the unforgiving pavement below. Just like my foolish hero, I had become more accustomed to failure than success. In the attempt, I showed questionable judgment and my choice resulted in intense, overwhelming pain. The wounds on my body were raw and blood was everywhere. Over time the pain subsided, replaced at first by aches and scabs, until the wounds finally healed. Eventually, all that was left to remind me of my adventurous foray into stunt riding were the scars.

Similarly, addiction came crashing into the lives of my family, and we found ourselves in an emotional pileup of drugs, blood, and guts. We suffered pain and emotional wounds that endure to this day. Our journey through addiction is easy to remember—but difficult to understand. The following pages are an attempt on my part to solve the puzzle of addiction by peeling back the layers and pulling off the scabs. What is addiction; how does it work; and how can it be beaten?

The current thinking on addiction reminds me of a famous book from the 19th century. Robert Louis Stevenson published his classic novel entitled *The Strange Case of Dr. Jekyll and Mr. Hyde* in 1886. In this wonderfully haunting narrative, Stevenson introduced a character named Dr. Henry Jekyll, a well- known physician who was determined to create a potion which would remove the darker sides of his personality. He was intent on finding a scientific means to isolate and effectively eliminate the defects in his character. Dr. Jekyll succeeded in creating this mixture and tested it on himself with disastrous results. Upon consuming the elixir, Jekyll transformed himself into an entirely different persona, the malevolent Edward Hyde. This disruptive alter-ego proceeded to run amok in Victorian London committing all sorts of atrocities, including murder. Even though Jekyll and Hyde are in reality the same person, the substance caused him to exhibit contradictory behaviors. In short, the story describes how a gentile, well-respected doctor was totally corrupted by deliberately consuming a substance of his own choosing.

Today's disease theory of addiction promotes a similar idea: presuming the addict to be corrupted in mind and body to such a degree that they lose the capacity for rational thought and the freedom of choice. Consuming drugs and alcohol, it is proposed, changes people in such a way as to render them helpless against the ravages of the so-called disease of addiction.

Is this an appropriate description of how addiction really works? Do the chemicals we ingest have total control over us, leading us entirely to the brink of our own destruction? Is it true that inside each one of us a Mr. Hyde is lurking? Let's find out.

The Root of the Problem

I've spent more than ten years researching the subject of addiction and numerous hours counseling people with addictive issues. Over the course of my investigation, I have reached a few major conclusions. I strongly believe that it is time someone stands in defense of those with addiction issues and speaks frankly with them regarding the underrated role of choice in the dependency process.

People don't need to hear more clinical talk or disease recovery excuses; they simply need someone to be honest with them about their situation. In counseling people with these issues, I have found them for the most part to be good people who have difficulty working through their problems. They are not inherently weak; they are simply guilty of making poor choices in response to their everyday circumstances.

In my experience, the addicted person is always aware (on some level) that he/she has a problem. However, they are reluctant to share this with others for fear of being labeled and judged. They resist assuming the damaged label of an "addict," even though their behavior speaks volumes in favor of the title. They feel alone; but they don't know why. Simply put, they need help.

What is the root of the problem? What is addiction, and how does it work? What are the physical characteristics of this so-called disease? Does it have a significant genetic component? What do the facts say about treatment; does it work? And finally, what roles do choice and free will play in diagnosing the so-called "disease" of addiction?

Addiction Facts and Figures

Overall, recent statistics suggest that addiction is becoming an ever more prominent concern in the U.S. today. According to recent surveys, approximately 22.6 million Americans age 12 and above were dependent on a substance in the previous year. That's nearly 10% of the overall U.S. population over the age of 12. Of those surveyed, 15.6 million people were dependent on alcohol and 3.8 million respondents were abusing illegal drugs. Overall, some 3.8 million people admitted to being dependent on both alcohol and illicit narcotics.[1]

All in all, approximately 30% of Americans claim to have some history of alcohol abuse, and around 10% have experience with drugs. In the year 2000, Americans were estimated to have spent more than $64 billion on illegal narcotics. At the same time, the United States government was spending about $12 billion per year on treatment and substance abuse programs.[2]

The federal government views addiction as a disease characterized by a loss of control in behavior, with a physiological cause that is independent of choice. The National Institute on Drug Abuse (a government funded addiction research center) has stated that addiction is "a brain disease beyond a reasonable doubt." Most treatment organizations, such as Alcoholics Anonymous (AA), share a similar viewpoint. While they sometimes advocate different approaches to a "cure," they all promote the disease model of addiction. Their fervid promotion of the disease theory of addiction has resulted in the general acceptance of this concept as the enlightened, mainstream view.[3]

CHAPTER TWO

Diagnosing the Disease
of Addiction

Science is the belief in the ignorance of the experts.
—Physicist Richard Feynman

THE MERRIAM-WEBSTER DICTIONARY defines the word *addiction* as follows: *"the compulsive need for and use of a habit-forming substance (such as heroin, or alcohol) characterized by tolerance and by well-defined psychological symptoms upon withdrawal."*[4]

In other words, an addiction is thought to be characterized by the use and/or abuse of a substance that has the ability to control certain aspects of human behavior. In most cases, the addictive substance is believed to alter the brain's chemistry in such a way as to make it irresistible to the user. Additionally, the substance itself is generally considered to be harmful to the overall well-being of the user. This definition describes the most generally accepted position that addiction is a disease that has been corrupting the minds of the general public for years.

The History of Substance Abuse

As a concept, addiction has a long and varied history. In fact, references to chemical abuse go back thousands of years. Alcohol has been around since the Stone Age, as purposely fermented beer jugs have been found dating back as far as 10,000 BC. In fact, the ancient Egyptians brewed beer in their homes and considered it to be a necessity of life. During the early modern period from 1500 to 1800 AD, the Catholic Church considered alcohol a "gift from God" to be used in moderation to promote good health.[5]

Narcotics, however, have a much more convoluted history. In the sixteenth century, laudanum (a mixture of opium and alcohol) began a rise to prominence in Europe and Asia. It was available in both pill and liquid form, and its hallucinogenic properties were quite potent. Users experimented with different additives, often substituting morphine for opium to achieve a more intense high. By the early 1800's, laudanum use in the upper classes was widespread, and the mixture had become identified as an "aristocratic vice."[6]

By the mid 19th century, opium use spread like wildfire in North America. When tens of thousands of Chinese laborers immigrated to the United States to work on the transcontinental railroad, they brought with them an affinity for smoking opium. This unhealthy vice spread quickly, taking root in railroad towns and mining camps in the American West. At this point, opium smokers were considered outsiders and the lifestyle that accompanied this abuse was generally considered to be socially unacceptable.[7]

At the dawn of the twentieth century, opium and alcohol usage increased and entered the realm of medical science. At the time, the vast majority of Americans had very little access to regular medical care. As a result, most people who became ill tended to medicate themselves rather than seek professional assistance. The treatments of choice were patent medications, whose active ingredients included alcohol, opiates, and even cocaine. In fact, individuals across the country could visit their local pharmacies and buy any combination of these so-called "miracle elixirs." They were even available for purchase by mail from Sears, Roebuck and Company and other national distributors. Interestingly, heroin was introduced at around the same time by the pharmaceutical giant Bayer as a highly effective cough suppressant.[8]

At this point, physicians in Europe began labeling self-destructive drug use a sickness. This theory built momentum and crossed the Atlantic, as it became a more prominent social issue. In the United States, the movement was initiated by Benjamin Rush (a signer of the Constitution) who believed that alcohol became a necessity as a function of drinking, itself. In his opinion, alcohol had the intrinsic ability to turn a voluntary drinker into an involuntary one.[9]

The newly formed Society for the Study and Cure of Inebriety embraced a similar position. Their Founder, Dr. Norman Kerr, stated their position as follows: "Inebriety is for the most part the issue of certain physical conditions... as unmistakably a disease as gout, or epilepsy, or insanity."[10]

As substance abuse evolved from a harmless personal habit into a significant criminal problem, the U.S. government felt the need to intercede. The Harrison Narcotics Act of 1914 was the result. This legislation limited the use of opiates and other addictive drugs to medical purposes only. The main thrust of the effort was based upon the assumption that drug abuse was primarily a criminal issue, not a medical one. It was enforced with vigor as if its intent was to suppress drug use and addiction entirely. As a result of this change in attitudes, American drug use patterns were completely transformed.[11] Narcotic use was thrust out of the public domain and into the shadowy margins of American society.

Operating on the assumption that individuals would not willingly choose to behave in a manner that was inherently self-destructive, the disease model of addiction was born. It was originally accepted as the proper way of describing alcoholism, but it has since been extended to apply to all other drugs. In most clinical texts, addiction is now introduced as a chronic illness that should be classified alongside diseases like asthma and diabetes. The U.S. government has even adopted this approach, and allocated its resources to that end. Generally speaking, the disease interpretation of addiction is now considered to be the scientific and enlightened perspective.[12]

The Contemporary View

The current disease model thinking is built upon a few important suppositions. First of all, it is believed that most addicts are in denial and do not think they have a problem worthy of concern. Dr. Gerald May, a well-known psychiatrist and addiction counselor, explains the concept.

> *During the early stages of the development of chemical addiction, the conscious mind studiously ignores or rejects any signs of increasing use of the substance. Not only does the person not recognize that a problem exists, he/she does not want to think about it. This is denial.*[13]

The second main tenet of the disease concept is the assertion that addicts lack complete control over their behavior when they use. This belief hinges upon the assumption that drug/alcohol abuse changes the chemistry within the brain and hinders the ability of the user to stop using. Individuals, in effect, become powerless over their addiction and lack the conscious control to stop using. In this case, it is thought that biology is the primary force that drives the addictive behavior.

Finally, addiction is considered to be a chronic illness that can sometimes be treated but never eliminated. Addicts are considered to be afflicted with a disease that will affect them throughout the course of their lifetime. The condition is assumed to have a genetic component that has given rise to the saying, "Once an addict... always an addict." Dr. Harold Urschel III, a prominent addiction specialist, explains this concept in a passage from his recent bestselling book, *Healing the Addicted Brain:*

> *Like diabetes, asthma, and other chronic diseases, addiction is a lifelong illness. Your diabetes is not cured simply because you're taking your medicine and watching your diet; it may be controlled, but it's still present. It's the same with the disease of addiction; it can be controlled but never completely eliminated.*[14]

It should be evident by now that addiction is widely viewed as a disease. This fact reminds me of a simple story that I recall from my time as an undergrad at Syracuse University. In my freshman year, I had made little progress toward choosing a major, as I spent most of my time pursuing a persistent state of intoxication. So I took quite a few different courses looking for something that might interest me in the long run. One of these classes was "Philosophy 101," which was taught by a young, disheveled Associate Professor named Mike. The class was tedious and boring for the most part, but I'll remember something that he said for as long as I live.

Professor Mike walked into class one day looking like he had just rolled out of bed and asked what I considered to be an odd question. "If you call a dog's tail a leg," he asked, "then how many tails does a dog have?" The entire class sat in stunned silence for a moment, and before anyone had a chance to respond he blurted out the answer. "The answer is four," he remarked with a grin. "It doesn't matter what you call it—the only thing that matters is what it is!"

CHAPTER THREE

Addiction and the Emperor's New Clothes

Sometimes the idea that drugs (or any addictive activities) have the power to place you in a passive position may actually be a kind of emotional defense: a denial of the active nature of addiction.

—Dr Lance Dodes
Harvard Psychiatrist

I F THE SO-CALLED disease of addiction cannot be cured, what options do we currently have to treat it? There are all types of rehabilitation and recovery programs that have been in existence for years. While they've garnered much praise from society as a whole, most have been surprisingly ineffective. We'll begin our discussion with one of the oldest and most acclaimed programs in existence.

Alcoholics Anonymous was founded in 1935 by Bill Wilson and Dr. Bob Smith. Both individuals, having struggled with alcohol, worked together with other early members to create a comprehensive program for the ongoing treatment of the "disease." Their program is based upon the "Twelve Steps to Sobriety" presented in their 1939 book, *Alcoholics Anonymous: The Story of How More Than One Hundred Men Have Recovered from Alcoholism* (otherwise known as the "Big Book"). The mission statement from their web page (AA.com) is as follows:

Alcoholics Anonymous® is a fellowship of men and women who share their experience, strength and hope with each other that they may solve their common problem and help others to recover from alcoholism. … Our primary purpose is to stay sober and help other alcoholics to achieve sobriety.[15]

The AA concept involves attending regular meetings with other alcoholics to discuss the disease and its shortcomings. Members are encouraged to attend these gatherings as often as possible in order to build a level of trust and camaraderie among attendees. New members choose a sponsor from within their group to serve as a sounding board for problems. In this way, members who have been in the program and been sober for some time sponsor newer members. They attempt to pass along the lessons of their own experiences, and hold the addicted person accountable for his/her actions.

The entire AA program is built on the foundation of the disease model of addiction. The "Big Book" states that the alcoholic has lost the power of choice, and thus has no defense against taking the next drink. One compelling twist is that the Twelve Step AA cycle requires members to abandon their ever-present denial and to turn their desires and will over to a so-called "higher power." Since AA is not affiliated with a particular religion, it is not specific as to what this higher power represents. In fact, I once heard an AA member comment that he had no concept of what his higher power was. He said that it may as well be a "doorknob," as long as he could surrender his will to it.

While AA is by no means a perfect program, it does exhibit certain qualities that seem to be helpful to addicts. It encourages members to be honest with themselves about the current state of their problems. It often energizes members by counting days of sobriety, which can motivate people to fight through particularly difficult times. When it works best, it offers a level of mutual support for alcoholics that can be valuable to an individual's long-term recovery.

The main problem with AA and its derivatives, however, lies in the fact that it doesn't seem to be particularly effective in a broad sense. While AA boasts of having more than 2 million members worldwide, many studies of the program have found that its members don't necessarily achieve sobriety more often than other alcoholics. For instance, two studies found (during 18 month follow-up interviews) that no more than 25% of people exposed to AA were still attending regular meetings. Of the attendees, only 22% were able to consistently maintain their sobriety. Taken together, both of these numbers indicate that fewer than 6% of AA members both attended meetings regularly and stayed sober.[16]

Stanton Peele, a well-known researcher in the field of addiction, reached the following conclusion is his book, *The Diseasing of America*:

> *Not one study has ever found AA or its derivatives to be superior to any other approach, or even to be better than not receiving any help at all for eliminating alcoholism when alcoholics are assigned to different kinds of treatment.*[17]

Statistically speaking, participating in AA affords alcoholics no better chance of conquering addiction than doing absolutely nothing at all.

Does Treatment Work?

Recent estimates have shown that Americans spend close to $20 Billion per year on professional treatment for alcohol and drug problems.[18] If a much acclaimed program like AA is not particularly effective, what results might we expect from the addiction treatment industry as a whole?

> *Surprisingly, the success rate for addiction treatment currently rests between 20 and 30%. In other words, 7 out of 10 Americans who participate in professional recovery programs experience relapse within a short period of time.*[19]

This is a mind blowing statistic. These success rates are substantially low considering the amount of money spent on research and rehabilitation. In fact, more money continues to be spent each year on treatment; despite the fact that most treatment programs are largely ineffective. We all know so-called addicts who have been in treatment several times, only to fall back into the same cycle of abuse shortly thereafter. Industry specialist Dr. Jeffrey Schaler surmises:

Addiction treatments do not work. This doesn't mean that individuals never give up their addiction after treatment. It's simply that they don't seem to do so at any higher rate than without treatment. One treatment tends to be just about as effective as any other treatment, which is just about as effective as no treatment at all.[20]

These startling facts beg the following question: Why doesn't treatment work? How is it that a vast majority of people who are treated professionally for the disease of addiction are seemingly not being "cured?"

The answers to this question may lie within the framework of the disease concept, itself. *Addicts are presumed to have failed at recovery because of the quality of their choices, but they suffer from a disease that allegedly impedes choice.* Dr. William Playfair, in his book entitled *The Useful Lie,* makes this point succinctly:

> *It (the disease model) introduces an exceedingly frustrating paradox. People are told they have a disease that prevents them from exercising self-control in their drinking habits, but that they must exercise self- control by totally abstaining from alcohol in order to keep from succumbing to the disease.*[21]

This reasoning makes little sense. Either choices matter or they don't… it can't be both. If choice and free will are relevant in this discussion, then the disease concept of addiction stands on shaky ground. Dr. Playfair says it best:

> *The alcoholism and drug recovery industry has a great deal to lose if the word gets out that this "disease" notion is the moral equivalent of the Emperor's new clothes. If there is no disease, then there is nothing to treat.*[22]

CHAPTER FOUR

Addiction and Physiology

People who drink to drown their sorrows should be told that sorrow knows how to swim.

—Ann Landers

THE DISEASE THEORY of addiction is so widely accepted that it has become part of the social fabric of America. People rarely question this idea, and they often support it without really understanding it. They know little about the contributing physiological factors beyond what they've been told by the mainstream media. They rely entirely on the opinions and suppositions of the experts in the field. In the case of addiction, the authorities in the field are typically physicians. Generally speaking, the mainstream public will often agree with a doctor's message out of simple respect for the messenger. Consequently, many people believe that addiction is a disease because doctors say it is.

In order to discover the truth, we must first identify what a disease actually is. Once we understand this, we can begin to critically examine the concept of addiction as a whole. Generally speaking, diseases are categorized into three main groups. These categories define the physical characteristics of the disorders and explain the nature of the affliction, itself.

The first category of diseases are disorders that are known for their physical manifestations, such as tuberculosis, aids, or cancer. These diseases have symptoms that can be measured in terms of concrete physiology. For instance, cancer is a disease that carries with it identifiable characteristics and predictable consequences. These first generation disorders are easily described in biological terms and are reasonably consistent in their symptomatic effects.[23]

The second category of diseases are primarily considered to be disorders of a psychological nature, the so-called mental illnesses. For the most part, this category describes disorders of the mind, such as bipolar disorder or schizophrenia. This type of disease is not identified by its physical symptoms, but by the feelings and emotions that are exhibited in the patient. These illnesses can be difficult to diagnose, and their symptoms can vary widely from one person to another. Second generation diseases are not typically exposed in medical tests or clinical brain scans.[24]

The third category of diseases is known exclusively by the behaviors they describe. Unlike mental illnesses (which are classified by disorderly thoughts), this category of illness is diagnosed entirely on the basis of its behavioral characteristics.[25] There are no identifiable biological characteristics of third generation diseases like those that manifest in other categories of disease. It is impossible to determine whether or not an individual has been afflicted with a third generation disease based solely upon the presence of physical symptoms.[26]

Addiction is commonly categorized as a third generation disease. People cannot be diagnosed with the "disease of addiction" in the absence of ongoing behavior. There are no telltale symptoms of the disease, like the ones that appear in cases of cancer or diabetes. There is no blood test that identifies addiction in individuals, and there is no evidence to suggest that people classified as addicts are born biologically different from anyone else. Dr. Schaler makes a critical observation:

> *A simple test of a true physical disease is whether it can be shown to exist in a corpse. There are no bodily signs of addiction itself (as opposed to its effects) that can be identified in a dead body. Addiction is therefore not listed in standard pathology textbooks.*[27]

The Biology of Addiction

In order to fully understand the intricacies of addiction, we need a brief lesson on the workings of our body's central nervous system. This is the network (governed by the brain) which coordinates our thoughts, actions, and emotions. The efficiency of this system depends on an interconnected array of billions of elements called neurons. These neurons are microscopic nerve cells that send and receive electrical nervous system data.

Our neurons are in constant communication with other neurons by way of chemical messages called neurotransmitters. These biochemical messages travel back and forth delivering information throughout the brain. When the system is working well, these messages travel between neurons with efficiency, creating thoughts in our mind that control our psychological well-being.

According to contemporary research, a neurotransmitter called dopamine is greatly affected by drug use. This organic chemical is primarily responsible for the regulation of our ability to move and to moderate emotions. Dopamine has also been found to enhance the expectation of pleasure and euphoric feelings in human beings.

Drugs and alcohol greatly influence the amount of dopamine in the central nervous system and the efficiency of its absorption by the neurons. Harvard psychologist Gene Heyman explains:

> *Neuron excitability and neuron to neuron communications are mediated by chemicals. Drugs are chemicals. Thus, drugs can alter neuron excitability and communication. … Cocaine promotes the functionality of dopamine, a neurotransmitter that mediates movement and motivation. These actions have a common end. They alter neuron excitability and neurons capacity to release and respond to neurotransmitters. Hence, psychoactive drugs alter perception, mood, awareness and action.*[28]

As intoxicating chemicals are consumed, the central nervous system is flooded with increased levels of dopamine, creating pleasurable sensations that the user wants to prolong. In order for the psychoactive high to persist, the user needs to continue "using." In basic terms, dopamine is the engine that powers the vehicle of addiction and intoxicating chemicals are the fuel.

Withdrawal and Physical Addiction

After an extended period of substance abuse, many individuals attempt to stop using through simple abstinence. The problem is that by then their bodies have become accustomed to the elevated dopamine levels in the brain. As a result, they can experience a variety of physical and psychological changes when they stop using. These reactions are biological indications that the body is compensating for the lack of the drug, which is a phenomena known as withdrawal. This process can be very uncomfortable for the addict, and sometimes extremely dangerous. Most treatment facilities try to mitigate these effects by slowly weaning their patients from their substance of choice in order not to shock their system and exacerbate the withdrawal process.

Taking this phenomenon into consideration, does this mean that addiction is purely a physical problem? The simple answer is "no." People who are detoxified and chemically "clean" often relapse in very short order. If they've abstained long enough to outlast the withdrawal process, then they cannot blame a physical addiction for choosing to resume the behavior. Harvard psychiatrist Dr. Lance Dodes explains:

> *How important to their (your) addiction is physical addiction? The first thing to be said about this is the most obvious. Detoxifying (withdrawing) people who are physically addicted to their drugs does not cure them. Not only do people often relapse immediately after detoxification, but it is well known that addictive behavior frequently returns even many years after the last drug use. Clearly, the essence of the addiction exists separately and independently from the presence of physical effects brought about by the drug itself, or by withdrawal from the drug.*[29]

In other words, the physical effects of withdrawal have generally dissipated within a few days or weeks after the cessation of use. This fact does not, however, stop the majority of addicts from relapsing within days, months, or even years. At this point, the physical attraction of the substance has waned, and the decision to resume its use must be associated with other factors.

Furthermore, many people are addicted to substances that are biologically incapable of producing physical addiction, such as marijuana or LSD. These types of drugs do not possess the chemical capability to create a biological urge for sustained use. While their hallucinogenic effects are undeniable, they cannot create the physically addictive symptoms of other categories of drugs. People who abuse these drugs are undoubtedly drawn to the psychoactive sensations that accompany them, but there is not a genuine physical addiction with which to contend.

Now that we have a basic understanding of how addiction works in our bodies, we must consider the overall importance of these physical factors. We have examined the workings of the central nervous system, which functions the same way in all of us. Alcohol, for instance, affects all users in similar ways, as it changes levels of dopamine in our brains. *If our nervous systems are all basically the same, and the chemical effects of abusing drugs and alcohol are virtually the same, then why don't we all become alcoholics when we drink?*

If biology is the primary driving force in addiction, then we would all become alcoholics and addicts upon exposure to intoxicating chemicals. Since this is clearly not the case, other factors must be considered. This fact strongly indicates that addiction cannot be characterized strictly in physical terms. While the brain undoubtedly reacts to the presence of drugs and alcohol in the body, the importance of physical addiction has been greatly exaggerated.

I remember a particular day from my childhood as though it was yesterday. I can still picture the view from our apartment window onto the parking lot in front of our building. This was the day I had long awaited... a day that had all the excitement of a birthday and Christmas wrapped up in one tiny package. My baby brother, who was born just days before, was coming home from the hospital. I was six years old, and I had wanted a little brother for as long as I could remember.

My younger sister and I stood anxiously near the front door of our modest apartment in West Virginia. My father passed away five years earlier, and our mother had remarried in 1974. My new brother Kevin Mason was born on September 30, 1975. Although I knew of his existence, I wanted to see him with my own eyes. My parents rolled into the lot in their '72 Gran Torino and carried the precious little bundle over the threshold.

There were "oohs" and "aahs" to spare, as we got our first look at the new addition to the family. We all got to hold him, and I got my first real taste of "brotherhood" in the changes that accompany a newborn's presence in a household. I remember sneaking into my parents' bedroom during nap-time that day to watch his chest rise and fall in the rhythmic dance of sleep. The only difference between this package and the ones at Christmas was that when you unwrapped this one it might "pee" on you.

As a family, we couldn't have been much happier. My new Dad was great! Even though we were by no means wealthy, we never lacked for anything. My parents worked hard; and my brother, my sister, and I played hard. My siblings and I lived carefree, innocent lives that were blessed with peace and harmony.

CHAPTER FIVE

Disease or Not a Disease?
That is the Question!

A disease is something you have, a behavior is something you do.

—E. Fuller Torrey

I F THE ROLE of physical addiction has been exaggerated in disease concept thinking, what can be said about the importance of genetics? One major assumption lies at the heart of disease theory: people are born as addicts and will continue to bear this burden throughout their lifetime. The saying (referenced earlier), "Once an addict… always an addict" has become the mainstream view of addiction. The question is; does this claim have any scientific justification?

The answer is clear and unambiguous. There is no evidence whatsoever to support the fact that addiction has an overwhelmingly genetic component.[30] *No study has ever discovered any chemical or anatomical abnormalities that are present in addicts that account for their having developed an addiction.* Harvard psychiatrist Dr Lance Dodes confirms these findings:

> *The most important finding of research into a genetic role in alcoholism is that there is no such thing as a "gene for alcoholism." Nor can you directly inherit alcoholism.*[31]

As of yet, there has been no "EUREKA!" moment in the genetic study of addictions that has found an obvious hereditary link. For instance, various studies have shown that only 25% of fathers and 5% of mothers of alcoholics are drinkers themselves.[32] Surprisingly, this means that if you are an alcoholic, your parents are far less likely to have a drinking problem than you are.

What about the concept of increased susceptibility to addiction? This would include the supposition that alcoholism and drug abuse tends to "run in families." While this is a popular viewpoint, no genetic link has ever been discovered among generational studies of addicts that can be considered statistically significant. Beyond that, most instances of this familial correlation can be explained away in terms of environment. More specifically, the fact that someone is an addict because one or both of their parents was an addict likely has more to do with the environment in which they were raised than with their inherited DNA.

Even if a so-called "gene for addiction" was ever to be discovered, that would not mandate that everyone in possession of this genetic material would become an addict. For example, consider for the moment the genetic predisposition of individuals with red hair and fair skin tones. These inherited conditions of lighter skin and a greater propensity to sunburn are undeniably genetic in nature. These people may need to use caution when considering prolonged exposure to sunlight, but their susceptibility to sunburn is not considered a disease.

Finally, let's consider research involving addiction and identical twins. These siblings are born when a single fertilized egg splits, creating two separate individuals that are genetically identical. They are exact reproductions of one another, right down to their DNA. When identical twins have been the subject of addiction studies, they have generated some surprising results. For instance, the correlation for alcoholism between identical twins was found to average about 40%.[33]

This means that if one twin is an alcoholic, the other twin (with exactly the same DNA) is more likely not to be an alcoholic. Since the twins in the study are genetically identical, these results are counter-intuitive. The genetic suppositions of the disease model predict one outcome, but we find that contemporary research supports the opposite conclusion. Harvard psychologist Gene Heyman surmises:

> *The facts say that the pathway from DNA to addiction is indirect, with genes programming proteins that affect the probability of addiction rather than insuring that it does or does not occur. The same point is made by a more general consideration. We inherit genes; we do not inherit behaviors.*[34]

Additional Addiction Research

Having discussed the relative value of physiology in our understanding of addiction, we need to examine further research in order to begin building valid conclusions. What do the facts say with respect to addiction as a whole? Does the remaining data support the popular disease model, or do we need to begin searching for a new way to explain the mysteries of addictive behaviors?

First of all, it should be noted that current addiction research relies largely on addicts who are receiving some form of professional treatment. *The primary problem with using this group as the basis for justifying broad theoretical concepts is that less than one-third of all addicts seek treatment.* Recent research suggests that only 30% of people ever bring their substance abuse problems to the attention of a health professional. As a result, the claims made by theorists that addiction is a chronic disease are based primarily on populations that may be unrepresentative of addicts as a whole.[35]

Additionally, the vast majority of people who use an addictive substance one or more times never become addicted to it. In fact, research suggests that 95% of Americans were able to try narcotics on a limited basis without becoming addicted. The percentage of people who drink alcohol but do not become alcoholics is about 85%. Those are surprising numbers, when you consider the fact that most people believe that addiction is an uncontrollable disease with a distinct genetic predisposition.[36]

Furthermore, research data suggests that most addicts subdue their addictions as they grow older and face the varied obligations of adult living. Gene Heyman concurs:

> *The biographical accounts suggested that most addicts quit drugs by their early thirties, and the epidemiological data strongly support this suggestion. To be sure, addicts may possibly relapse the first few times they try to quit, but according to the surveys, by about age 30 most have quit for good. Thus, for addiction, quitting drugs is more accurately described as "resolution," not "remission," when the ex-drug user is more than 30 years old.*[37]

This data suggests that most people simply evolve beyond their addictive tendencies and choose to embrace more mature, responsible alternatives. These facts are in no way consistent with the notion that addiction is a disease.

One final study of addiction involves a research project undertaken at the end of the Vietnam War. This psychological study examined the addictive behavior of more than 400 opiate-using soldiers returning from combat to the United States. These veterans had used opiates (mostly heroin) on a regular basis during the war. They all experienced withdrawal upon cessation of use and admitted they were addicted to the drugs. The stresses of combat had no doubt precipitated this abuse, and it was assumed that these men would continue to use opiates upon returning to America. *Surprisingly, no more than 12% of the soldiers who had been addicted in Vietnam continued to use opiates upon their return. More directly, nearly 9 out of 10 individuals stopped using the drug at home, despite their previous addiction in the war.*[38]

These results makes little sense in terms of the disease theory of addiction. If the physical effects of using heroin had the ability to control their behavior, then the individuals in the study would have continued in their addictions. If they were born addicts, their genetic predispositions would have required them to remain under the influence of the chemicals. If the drugs controlled them physically, then their behavior would never have changed. None of these findings are compatible within the framework of the disease concept. Dr. Lance Dodes settles the matter:

> *The result of this study of Vietnam veterans underscores a basic point. Addiction is a human problem that resides in people, not in the drug or in the drug's capacity to produce physical effects.*[39]

This is a very important connection to make. If a substance doesn't turn you into an addict and genetics are not to blame, then behavior and choice must play a much larger role than originally understood. Addiction researcher Stanton Peele agrees:

> *Disease conceptions of misbehavior are bad science and are morally and intellectually sloppy. Biology is not behavior, even in those areas where a drug or alcohol is taken into the body.*[40]

Taken as a whole, modern research on addiction suggests that the disease concept of addiction is not only flawed, but no longer valid. It is an outdated collection of theories and over-reaching assumptions that lack sound scientific justification. If addiction cannot be explained in terms of biology or genetics, then it must be examined as a function of behavior.

CHAPTER SIX

Addiction and the Power of Choice

What is wrong with disease theories as science is that they are tautologies; they avoid the work of understanding why people drink or smoke in favor of simply declaring these activities to be addictions, as in the statement "he drinks so much ...because he's an alcoholic."

—Stanton Peele

A TAUTOLOGY IS A statement that is redundant in nature. Because they depend upon the assumption that they are already correct, these self-reinforcing statements cannot be disproved. Stanton Peele clearly states that disease theories of addiction are tautologies because they depend on their own assumptions to confirm their validity. In simple terms, this makes about as much sense as saying, "Addicts will always be addicts... because they are addicts."

Perhaps the most damaging misconception in the disease concept of addiction lies within the statement above. AA, the media, and treatment providers today all proclaim with vigor that addicts are addicted—now and forever. People are informed of this grim prognosis from the very beginning of treatment. Many people are told they cannot ever have another drink because they are afflicted with the disease of alcoholism. Presumably, they are sick people who are burdened by the lifelong curse of addiction. They become convinced that because of this pathology, they will inevitably lose control over their dependent behaviors. The much-acclaimed principle of "denial" feeds this notion. Stanton Peele explains:

> *What if you are told you are an alcoholic and that you must abstain for life and you don't agree? Then you are, according to treatment wisdom, practicing denial. If, on the other hand, you continue to disagree with such diagnoses, then denial can then be used as evidence that you are really alcoholic or addicted.*[41]

The Self-Fulfilling Prophecy

You've been told for years by the prevailing wisdom that you are burdened with a disease and you cannot control your own behavior. After a while, you begin to accept this diagnosis and feel justified in exhibiting the symptoms of the disease. *You begin to rationalize your destructive behavior in the context of your new-found sickness. You naturally begin to accept your fate thinking, "If I'm going to be treated like an addict, I may as well act like one."* In this way, addiction for many people becomes a self-fulfilling prophecy. The following illustration by addiction specialist Dr. Abraham Twerski makes this point succinctly:

> *Suppose you had an automobile that was operating well, but a part became defective. You would replace the defective part and the car would run well again. If, however, you found your car was a "lemon" and each time you corrected a problem something else went wrong, you might throw your hands up in disgust. You might justifiably conclude there is no purpose in getting the car repaired. This is what happens in addictive thinking. The profound shame that addicts feel results in their thinking that it is futile to change their ways.*[42]

The bottom line is this—the more confidence people have in their ability to break a cycle of addiction, the more successful they can be in doing so. Stanton Peele concurs:

Cultural and historic data indicate that believing alcohol has the power to addict a person goes hand in hand with more alcoholism. For this belief convinces susceptible people that alcohol is stronger than they are, and that—no matter what they do—they cannot escape its grasp. What people believe about their drinking affects how they react to alcohol.[43]

Dr. Jeffrey Schaler takes the thought one step further:

The more people believe in their ability to moderate their consumption of drugs and alcohol, the more likely they will be to moderate. The converse is also true: the more people believe in their inability to moderate their consumption of drugs and alcohol, the more likely they will be not to moderate.[44]

If you are told by someone in a position of authority that you cannot do something, how hard will you then try to do it? If you believe what you've been told by disease proponents, you may well surrender in battle before the war even begins. The famed industrialist Henry Ford distilled this notion into one simple saying: "Whether you think you can or think you can't—You are right!" The bottom line is this—as long as people believe they cannot do something, they probably will be unable to do it.

The Final Nail in the Coffin

The concept of addiction as a disease hinges on one final assumption. The fact that people use chemicals to create pleasurable sensations is obvious and indisputable. The fact that abusing these substances can cause numerous health problems and/or death cannot be argued against. Disease model proponents have taken these two facts and twisted them into the following supposition: addicts will not willingly choose to continue behavior that is blatantly self-destructive. Gene Heyman explains:

Since addiction is self-destructive, the logical implication is that addicts cannot be voluntarily choosing to use drugs. Since the symptoms of the disease are involuntary, then addiction must be a disease. In other words, medical evidence did not turn alcoholism into a disease, but rather the assumption that voluntary behavior is not self-destructive turned alcoholism into a disease.[45]

Once again, we find that disease theory makes little sense in the context of typical human behavior. People (like my hero Evel Knievel) make questionable decisions quite often, some of which result in life threatening consequences. They sky dive and bungee jump—they even wrestle alligators for sport. None of these activities are inherently safe, yet they are not categorized as diseases. Gene Heyman elaborates:

> *Research on drug use implies that individuals repeatedly make choices that are not in their long-term interests and that they themselves often regret. Laboratory and natural setting experiments reveal that individuals make their choices on the basis of the current values of the available items. Depending on the experimental conditions, this can lead to serious sub-optimal outcomes. ... Nevertheless, the population trends and lever pressing rate tell the same story: choice tends to produce less than optimal outcomes. Addiction is a disorder of choice.*[46]

Overall, the disease concept of addiction falls apart upon close inspection. Physical addiction is not an irresistible force that drives addictive behaviors. There are no direct genetic links among addicts that condemn them to a lifetime of substance abuse. Contemporary research shows that most people are able to try drugs or alcohol without becoming addicted, a fact clearly reinforced by the Vietnam heroin study. Finally, research shows that most people outgrow their addictions, choosing sobriety as an alternative to the anarchy of dependency. This leads me to believe that conscious choice and alternatives play a much greater role than previously imagined.

Do chemicals control you, or do you control them? Deep within your heart you know the answer.

CHAPTER SEVEN

Addiction and Pleasure: Partners in Crime

The greatest harm most people experience is the result of what they do to themselves.

—Stanton Peele

HAVING DEFINED CHOICE as perhaps the most important factor in driving addictive behaviors, it is important to explore the subject in greater detail. Specifically, why do people make poor choices? What factors make chemicals so irresistible that they choose them over family, finances, and even their own health?

Cocaine does not leap into our noses, nor does alcohol force itself down our throats. At this point, we need not be concerned with the effects of the drugs once ingested. Instead, we must carefully identify the processes that allowed them to enter the body in the first place. The motives behind these deliberate choices will tell the true tale of addiction.

Pressure and stress are inevitable in everyday life. This is no more obvious than in the lives of drug and alcohol abusers. Lifestyle and recreational choices only add fuel to the fire of the intense anxieties of human existence. Despite these conditions, an addict's free will and ability to choose remain in force. They may feel compelled to use chemicals, but are in no way required to do so. Dr. Gerald May concurs:

> *No matter how oppressed we are, by other people and*
> *circumstances or by our own internal addictions, some small*
> *capacity for choice remains unvanquished.*[47]

Along these lines, I believe that the phenomena of pleasure seeking is greatly underestimated in modern addiction theory. The substances in question (alcohol and potent narcotics) are ingested because of their psychoactive properties. These chemicals create feelings of euphoria, considerably altering our perceptions of life in the moment. Addicts are undeniably chasing the hallucinogenic properties of the 'high.' In simple terms, the addict becomes addicted to the experience, itself. Stanton Peele elaborates:

> *Rather than losing control of their drinking, experiments*
> *show alcoholics aim for a desired state of consciousness when*
> *they drink. They drink to transform their emotions and their*
> *self-image—drinking is a route to achieve feelings of power,*
> *sexual attractiveness, or control over unpleasant emotions.*
> *Alcoholics strive to attain a particular level of intoxication,*
> *one that they can describe before taking a drink.*[48]

Without a doubt, basic human nature drives us to to seek pleasure whenever possible. In the United States, we are even constitutionally guaranteed the right to "life, liberty, and the pursuit of happiness." This is not a new concept. However, addicts seem to place a greater emphasis on pursuing pleasure and intoxicating sensations. Dr. Jeffrey Schaler explains:

> *Addiction is a fondness for, or orientation toward, some thing*
> *or activity, because it has meaning, because it is considered*
> *valuable or even sacred. In some cases, people may be addicted*
> *to something because they find it enjoyable, and this, of course,*
> *also reflects their values: such a person believes that the right*
> *way to live is to seek enjoyment.*[49]

Pleasure seeking and gratification are easy concepts to understand, and they drive behavior in addicts more so than any other factor.

Addictive Thinking

It has been suggested that addicts think differently than everyone else; that chemicals control their ability to consciously choose. I respectfully disagree. In my opinion, the thought processes of addicts are identifiable and quite predictable. They deliberately control their own thoughts and actions in order to achieve a desired state.

For instance, some have been told for years that as alcoholics, they are unable to resist a drink. So when life gets intense, they predictably "want a drink" to escape the reality of their current situation. This desire for a drink is then processed internally and transformed into "needing a drink" as a function of their supposed disease. Since they allegedly cannot be expected to suppress this "compulsion," they take the steps necessary to get a drink. They follow a natural, logical process to determine that nothing in the present moment has more value than indulging in an alcoholic beverage.

As a result, addicts often have considerable trouble regulating their own activities. Focusing on their own needs, they fail to consider the effects their behavior will have on others. Intent on satisfying these "compulsive" urges, they seem to show total disregard for the concerns of friends and family. Many addicts are so focused on their substance of choice that their habits take precedence over familial responsibilities. Baby formula becomes less important than whiskey. Child support falls by the wayside in favor of supporting a heroin habit. Oddly enough, if you ask an addict what is most important to them, they will invariably answer, "my family." Ironically, the evidence of their actions does not support this claim.

Most addicts eventually make their choices out of pure self-indulgence. They believe that these addictive substances will soothe their feelings and remove the pain. While they do briefly feel better, the inevitable pains of life seemingly creep back into view. Dr. Lance Dodes explains:

> *If you are feeling discouraged and find yourself turning to a drug or another addictive act with the feeling that it will 'take care' of you, it is helpful to know that this is an illusion. You are taking care of you, or at least trying to, via the addictive act.*[50]

When you engage in an addictive behavior, you are doing everything you can at that moment to help yourself. In other words, *"No one loves you... like you!"* Inevitably, drunkenness and drug abuse are the unfortunate consequences.

The good news is that your capacity for choice remains undisturbed. If you can choose to make bad choices, then you can alternately choose to make good ones. You may not have a history of making rational decisions, but the past has no value other than what we can learn from it. Your current life may be reigned by wreckage, but things can turn around very quickly. Gene Heyman concludes:

> *Addicts quit outside the purview of clinics, which is what one would expect if the matters of everyday life are what brought drug use to a halt. Biographical, epidemiological, ethnographic, and clinical research led to the same conclusion: addicts are not compulsive drug users. They choose to keep using drugs, and they can, and do, choose to quit.*[51]

Personal Responsibility is Key

So, where does this leave us? We are attempting to take an important leap from the dark valley of denial into the luminous land of personal responsibility. You alone are ultimately responsible for the choices you make! You alone determine the path you choose from the divergent options of addiction and sobriety! Dr. Lance Dodes agrees:

> *An object of addiction does not magnetically attract you— you are the one who supplies the magnetism. The good news about this, of course, is that it means you also may control the process once you understand it.*[52]

It is vital that you begin to take personal responsibility for your self-destructive addictive behaviors. If you've been drinking too much—take responsibility! If you've been abusing drugs—take responsibility! If you've been living a life other than the one you'd imagined—take responsibility! When addicts start to take ownership of their choices, they take the first step in the process of regaining control of their lives. Admittedly, this is easier said than done. But it can absolutely be done.

Don't forget that around 85% of all people who try drugs and alcohol never become addicts. So the vast majority of people are able to remain free of the grip of addiction. Why is this true? What is different about those people? Values seem to play an important role in answering these questions. Stanton Peele elaborates:

> *The role of people's value-driven choices is ignored in descriptions of addiction. The reasons that these and other people do not become drug addicts are all values issues—the people don't see themselves as addicts, don't wish to spend their time pursuing and savoring the effects of drugs, and refuse to engage in certain behaviors that might endanger their family lives or careers. Without question, values are crucial in determining who becomes and remains addicted or who chooses not to do so.*[53]

Remember—you choose where you live; you choose what company you keep; and you choose how you respond to stress and problems in living. In order to make better choices, you need to start making changes in what you believe. Stanton Peele comments:

> *We have seen across the range of addictions that it takes both an intrapsychic change—or a reconceptualization of who you are, what is good for you, and how you wish to live—and real life changes to bring off quitting an addiction.*[54]

In this world, change may be the only constant. Change is not something to fear, but staying the same might be.

The look on his face was priceless. My little brother couldn't have looked more pitiful or surprised if I had reached out and slapped him in the face. I remember with retrospective delight seeing the elevator doors closing between us in all the glory of its slow motion hilarity.

The year was 1984, and we were on a family vacation in Washington, DC. After a day of sightseeing, we parked the car and headed for the hotel elevators. We all piled into the elevator ... well *almost* all of us. Somehow, my brother Kevin had fallen behind and been "shut-out" of the elevator before anyone could stop the doors from closing. I can still see the image in my mind of this bewildered young boy disappearing slowly out of view between the elevator doors.

When the doors refused to open despite the frantic attempts of my parents, my sister and I howled with laughter as we began the deliberate climb to the lobby. We were chastised for our outburst by our parents, who were understandably distressed by the sober reality of the moment. Their nine year old son had been unceremoniously banished from our presence by the evil elevator doors! He had, after all, been left alone in a parking garage in one of the most dangerous cities in America!

Upon arriving at the lobby level, we pressed the down buttons furiously and eventually succeeded in getting the elevator back to the parking deck. When the doors finally parted, there stood my brother Kevin with exactly the same look of astonishment on his face. He didn't cry, he didn't panic, and he never moved from that spot. Having gathered him in and averted disaster, we were afforded a hearty laugh at his expense.

Although I tormented him endlessly, Kevin took it all in stride. He was always a tough kid, having endured the regular abuse of his elder siblings. Over the years, we would grow to be as close as two brothers can get.

This funny little story serves as an innocent appetizer to the meal that life would soon serve us. As a family, we would need all of the toughness that we could muster in order to navigate the obstacles accompanying Kevin's eventual substance abuse.

CHAPTER EIGHT

Addiction and Common Sense

The simplest explanation for some phenomenon is more likely to be accurate than more complicated explanations.

—Occam's Razor
Law of Physics

OCCAM'S RAZOR IS a scientific principle attributed to the 14th century logician Friar William of Occam. The theory states that the simplest explanation for complex phenomena is the best. Without a doubt, addiction can at the very least be characterized as a "complex phenomena." It has been studied by scientists and public institutes for years, resulting in the convoluted theory of addiction as a disease. But as we discussed earlier, just because you call a dog's tail a "leg" doesn't necessarily make it so.

It seems as if AA and the treatment community have stubbornly embraced the outdated disease theory of addiction, and now they spend most of their time and effort trying to support it with concrete facts. This goes against the established methods of scientific study and theoretical medicine. One should consider the facts and examine behaviors first, and then build a theory of addiction that conforms to the observable data.

Who you are and what you do matters most in terms of plotting a course toward sobriety. As a result, I have developed a simpler model that fits more appropriately within the parameters of chemical addiction. On the basis of personal research and that of professionals in the field, the following has been concluded: addiction is not a disease. Addiction is simply the result of a set of sub-optimal choices that manifest themselves in the form of self-destructive behaviors.

This new concept, which I call the Common Sense Model of Addiction (CSM), is a more direct collection of ideas that fit the facts and data that describe addiction today. This model may be controversial, but it has evolved out of the respect and compassion that I feel for individuals who are hanging from the addiction cliff of life. The following principles are addressed to those very people.

THE COMMON SENSE MODEL OF ADDICTION (CSM)

1) **You are a person, not an "addict."**
2) **You alone have the power of choice.**
3) **Addiction is often an excuse for problems in living.**
4) **Rock Bottom is a dangerous concept.**
5) **Maturity and responsibility are the enemies of addiction.**
6) **Environment is crucial in addiction recovery.**
7) **Spiritual help is invaluable in overcoming addiction.**

Let's examine each of these principles in greater depth and discover how they can help contribute to your personal growth and sobriety. Each point is presented with a real life example of someone who most strikingly exhibits the principle in question. All the names have been changed to protect the privacy of the individuals in question.

Principle 1: You are a person, not an "addict."

This may be the most important concept for you to understand. It impacts and affects the way you perceive yourself and relate to others. Once you grasp this concept, it will empower you and greatly improve the manner in which you respond to future problems. The disease model (proposed by the recovery industry) has labeled you an "addict born with the disease of addiction." You've been told it's like an infection that entered your body and wreaks havoc in your brain, controlling your thoughts and behaviors in the process.

Disease theory says you live in denial of your problems, but I respectfully disagree. In my experience, most addicts are well aware of their substance abuse problems. They simply avoid admitting them to others, primarily to keep from being labeled an "addict." The cultural and social stigmas that come with this label can be very difficult to shed.

The fact is that there is nothing different (biologically or genetically) about you that condemns you to a lifetime of dependency. You may have made poor choices in the past, but everyone is guilty on that charge. You are not a slave to drugs or alcohol! You should embrace this fact and attempt to take control of your thoughts and actions.

Phillip is a man in his early twenties who began struggling with an addiction to painkillers after an automobile accident in his early teens. He is a respectful young man and lives in a supportive family environment. Since we met years ago, he has suffered a number of substance related seizures that nearly resulted in death. Phillip has been in and out of treatment quite a few times, but he never seemed to make any progress. He's been told for years by the recovery industry that he will always be an addict, a fact that he enthusiastically embraces.

In the past, Phillip often used the disease label as an excuse for his behavior. Recently, he has begun to understand that he alone determines whether or not he is an addict based on the quality of his conduct. He has progressed in his recovery to the point where he is focused on taking personal responsibility for his choices, which has made all the difference in the world.

Principle 2: You alone have the power of choice.

Are you Dr. Jekyll or Mr. Hyde? Do the potions you ingest take total control of your mind and body, turning you into a different, darker person altogether? Of course not and you know it! No substance on earth has the ability to completely control your choices. If you're willing to view your actions objectively, you'll come to understand that every single choice you've made (for better or for worse) has belonged to you. The upside of this realization is tied directly to your ability to change your life by making better, more beneficial decisions.

Many addicts whom I have counseled in the past have broken through their vices and experienced the serenity associated with sobriety. Most have taken ownership of their choices—realizing that no one else is to blame. They took personal responsibility for their actions and embraced the opportunity to use the power of choice to break free from the "slavery" of addiction.

Evan is a young man entering has late twenties with a history of heroin abuse. He once told me an unforgettable story. He was squatting in a condemned property that had been completely overrun by heroin and crack addicts. He says he was in the midst of a heroin fueled binge when he lost consciousness and nearly died. Just days before, he had jokingly told his fellow drug users what to do if he should ever overdose. He said they should just drag him outside with the trash and leave him. Regretfully, he awoke from this latest binge to find himself outside lying next to a dumpster in a pile of garbage. His "drug buddies" had taken his flippant suggestion to heart.

Evan is currently experiencing his first sober months in years, mostly as a result of a return home to his family. Life for Evan is not perfect, but the stresses of home seem minimal compared to the horrific nightmare of life on the streets. When asked how he found himself in this position, he will admit that all of the consequences of his substance abuse came as a result of his own deliberate choices. He admits to even choosing heroin at the expense of time spent with his newborn daughter. Evan is currently employed and is well on his way to a life filled with promise rather than one on the edge of addictive destruction.

Principle 3: Addiction is often an excuse for problems in living.

It is an undeniable fact that many people abuse substances as a means of detaching from the problems of everyday life. I've met individuals with horrific personal histories, ranging from physical abuse to sexual molestation. If you have ever suffered similar circumstances, these issues need to be addressed! However, you cannot allow these tragic events to assume a position of power in your life, serving as a convenient excuse for self-destructive behaviors.

Tony is a young man fresh out of his teens with a serious marijuana problem. After being arrested for drug possession, he came to my attention through the Drug Court Program. Since he had no prior criminal record, the court ordered requirement for having his record expunged was for him to stay drug free for six months. At one point, he passed five straight months of drug testing, only to fail the sixth and final test. This ruined his chances of graduating from the program. When asked why he smoked after such a long period of abstinence, he responded simply that he could not handle the stress in his life. His lack of effort to confront these issues was a major factor in his continuing use.

Tony and his family live in a poverty stricken area surrounded by environmental influences that made maintaining sobriety difficult. He and his family struggle financially, and he used these commonplace stresses as an excuse for prolonged drug use. His money problems, combined with chronic relationship issues, had forestalled his recovery.

Tony was eventually able to admit that the problems resulting from the aforementioned slip were no different from any he'd experienced in the past. He admits that he let his guard down and chose to revert back to a more comfortable, chemical response. He learned a valuable lesson from this minor lapse and is now moving forward with a new job and different relationships. His story is by no means unique in addiction circles.

As human beings, we all have problems… some more burdensome than others. We all must deal with the stresses of everyday life. However, we don't all feel the need to use chemicals to escape the pain—nor do we choose to function in a drug induced fog. If you feel like you have serious problem, guess what… you are not alone! Over the years, I've discovered that many of my problems came as a direct result of my own destructive choices. If you ignore your problems by self-medicating and feel sorry for yourself, it's time to STOP! Instead, begin to channel your energy toward more constructive efforts to solve the problems over which you have control.

Principle 4: Rock Bottom is a dangerous concept.

Many substance abusers are willing to take life's punches without lifting a hand in their own defense. They become so self-absorbed that they await the inevitable devastation to come with no real consideration for friends or family. They seem to be willing to wait until things get so serious that only two options remain—sobriety or death. This is a description of the phenomena known in addiction circles as hitting "rock bottom."

The idea that people can wait until they hit "rock bottom" is not only absurd but dangerous. This idea often encourages addicts to continue using chemicals until they feel they've reached this metaphorical "bottom"– one which is only identifiable after the fact. Since many people recognize their personal bottom in retrospect, this concept encourages the continuation of destructive behaviors until the emotional, relational, and physical decline prevails. At this point, these people seriously question the value of life, itself.

Through Drug Court, I became acquainted with a young man named Chuck. He's a bright individual who comes from a solid family. When I first saw him, he was wearing the all too familiar striped jumpsuit that comes with a prolonged stay in the county jail. He was arrested on a possession charge and entered our program hoping to have his record expunged.

Whenever I spoke with him, he never seemed to think that his situation was serious enough to consider making a change. A familiar pattern had developed in his life. He would get out of jail and stay clean and sober for a little while. Then he would inevitably go back to making irresponsible, chemical fueled choices. When I confronted him about this fact, he would always reply, "I guess I haven't hit rock bottom yet."

This notion of waiting for some mythical "bottom" had become an excuse for him to continue his destructive lifestyle. Even after six months in jail, he was never willing to admit that drugs had become more valuable to him than his very own freedom.

Simply put, when you've reached the point where using chemicals is less valuable to you than sobriety and life itself, you've hit rock bottom. Until then, you're placing more worth on intoxicating chemicals than you are on your very own existence. When the competing options that accompany sobriety become worth more to you than chemicals, you can begin the climb back to responsible living.

Principle 5: Maturity and responsibility are the enemies of addiction.

Are you aware that many female addicts are able to stop abusing drugs and alcohol during pregnancy? I've personally known a number of women who (although they had struggled significantly with drugs) were able to stop using them during pregnancy and give birth to healthy children. If addiction is a disease, how is that possible? Does the disease go into remission for nine months, only to flare up again after the birth of a child?

As previously stated, the vast majority of addicts are able to stop using substances by age 30. This age, as I recall, involves the unique transition from young adulthood to becoming a spouse, a parent, and a household provider. As we age, our corresponding responsibilities tend to increase. Gene Heyman explains:

> *According to biographies, financial and family concerns were among the main reasons addicts quit using drugs. Economic and financial responsibilities are also the concerns of adulthood. This suggests that the pressures that typically accompany "maturity" bring drug use to a halt in many addicts. ... Those with greater access to meaningful alternatives are more likely to quit using. This generalization is, of course, a way of saying that drug use in addicts is voluntary, or, put the other way around, addicts are not compulsive drug users; addiction is not a disease.*[55]

Research has shown that the majority of both men and women tend to outgrow their addictions as they assume the complex burdens of adulthood. Even though family and careers cause stress for us all, they tend to scare away the so-called disease of addiction!

When I first met Lisa, she was just coming off a stint in prison for a felony drug charge. She was incarcerated for 18 months in a woman's facility downstate and was looking for a brand new start. Prior to her arrest, she had abused crystal methamphetamine for more than twenty years. The drug had become an integral part of her lifestyle and affected all of her adult decisions.

In prison, she realized that (partly due to her age) she had more life experience than most of the women in her cell block. While incarcerated, she made an attitude adjustment that resulted in meaningful emotional change. She felt the need to share these new-found insights with her fellow inmates, becoming a mother-figure and a mentor of sorts. Upon her release, she returned home to a family that desperately needed her. She was determined not to fail them, so she resolved to stay clean. She found a group of close supporters and relied on them for encouragement and accountability. As of this writing, Lisa has been sober for more than three years. She credits her faith and her familial responsibilities with keeping her drug free.

Principle 6: Environment is crucial in addiction recovery.

Were you alone in your room when you first experimented with alcohol or illicit drugs? Probably not—and the majority of addicts will agree. Most people with serious substance abuse issues began "using" in their early teens. They often experimented with various substances at the urging of a group of friends or even family members.

If you began using chemicals in a group, you'll likely continue using socially as your addictive tendencies persist. What makes you think you can remain in this very same environment (with the very same people) and have any chance at all of changing your behavior?

People who abuse alcohol and drugs are often hesitant to make changes in their addictive environments. Addicts, like most people, are comfortable around familiar faces and in familiar places. Comfort, however, can be a deceiving emotion because it can mask the reality of addictive situations. If your environment has contributed to your addiction, then you need to let it contribute to your sobriety by changing it! I can give you very few examples of addicts who were able to get sober in the same environment that played a major role in their fall.

Bobby is a man in his mid-thirties that I met through Celebrate Recovery. He struggled mightily for ten years with an addiction to heroin. He grew up in a large city and developed his addictive habits among a core group of "user friends." His substance abuse eventually progressed to the point of potentially costing him his life. In a moment of clarity, he realized that saving his life depended on removing himself from this unhealthy environment. As a result, he made a life-changing decision to relocate to a different geographic area away from the former temptations that had contributed to his original downfall.

Bobby moved to another state in an attempt to distance himself from his former addictive environment. He got a new job, developed new friendships, and discovered a new-found lifestyle of sobriety. Life in his former hometown revolved around the culture of drug use, and he needed a deliberate change of scenery. From the moment he arrived in the new location, his actions and behavior were perceptibly different. He was miles away from his problems, both literally and figuratively. This example may seem a little extreme to some, but it offers valuable insight into the importance of a safe environment in achieving sustained sobriety.

Principle 7: Spiritual help is invaluable in overcoming addiction.

One of the most intriguing elements of the Alcoholics Anonymous (AA) program involves the role of a "higher power" in recovery. Step three of the "Twelve Steps" recommends that we "Make a decision to turn our will and our lives over to the care of God *as we understand Him*." (emphasis in the original). In general, this has become one of the most popular and controversial aspects of the program. Dr. Lance Dodes promotes its value:

> *Besides its quality as a mutual support, when it (AA) works best it relies on substituting an external omnipotent power for an addictive action—for instance, drinking. Members are encouraged to acknowledge that they have failed to be able to control their own lives, and to turn over their will to a higher power. ... AA is encouraging people to make a shift*

> *in their source of power and strength. When people can make*
> *use of this idea, they give up the addictive behavior which had*
> *produced a needed sense of mastery and control, and replace*
> *it with the AA concept of a higher power.*[56]

The AA concept of spirituality relies on a belief in an ambiguous "higher power." The organization goes to great lengths to ensure that it is not associated with a specific culture or religion. AA doesn't care what you believe… just that you believe in something beyond yourself.

On the other hand, I have unambiguous ideas as to the identity of this "higher power." In my view, the greatest advantage an addict can have in engineering a break in a cycle of addiction lies in an enduring faith in God.

Bobby, the same individual mentioned previously in this chapter, can attest to the value of spirituality in a journey from addiction to sobriety. He was taken in by relatives and given the opportunity to regularly attend church for the first time in his life. As a result of this exposure, he asked for complete deliverance from his addiction, and his prayers were answered. Amazingly, he never experienced any symptoms of heroin withdrawal (which are typically vicious in nature); he never fell into the fog of detoxification; and he has never looked back! As of this writing, he has been drug free for more than three years and is looking forward to celebrating another "birthday" in peace and sobriety.

CHAPTER NINE

Addiction and the Value of Spirituality

Addictive thinking is non-spiritual, since its goal is the polar opposite of spirituality.

—Dr. Abraham Twerski

PEOPLE LOVE TO pass judgment on other people and their behaviors. This is one of the most unfortunate, hypocritical elements of human nature. Most people judge addicts by incorrectly assuming them to be morally and spiritually bankrupt. Often those judging seem to revel in attaching derogatory labels to people (such as "drunk" or "junkie") based on their perception of the addicts behavior. All the while, they conspicuously ignore the glaring inconsistencies in their own conduct. On the contrary, I have found most addicts to be rather spiritual people. In fact, many pronounce a firm belief in God. The problem is that they don't seem to truly understand what that means.

I would never presume to judge anyone nor estimate someone's value as a person based on the quality of their choices. I am in no position to look down upon anyone, especially considering the questionable content of my own character as a young adult. I was a "drunk" for many years, until I matured and learned that alcohol was clouding my judgment and arresting my development into a responsible adult.

Nevertheless, there is one major point I want to emphasize. Your addiction does not affect your value as a person. You are not diseased, and you likely have no more psychological problems than your friends and neighbors. Harvard lecturer Dr. Lance Dodes agrees:

> *Contrary to what you have heard, suffering from an addiction in itself does not make you fundamentally psychologically "sicker" or less mature than people with a wide variety of other difficulties, who generally are not so harshly judged. The feelings and conflicts that underlie addiction are easily understandable in human terms and do not set you apart from anyone else.*[57]

I have profound respect for those of you that are constantly battling your chemical desires and fighting for sobriety. There is still some fight left in you, as evidenced by the fact that you are reading this book. You may be dangling from a cliff, but you haven't let go yet! But your behavior needs to change, and you know it!

In order to accomplish your dependency goals, I encourage you to make an immediate assessment of your current situation. Try to recognize your inclination to detach as a means of not responding to adverse circumstances (stress, financial issues, relationship problems, etc.) and acknowledge the consequences of those actions in your life. Hopefully, you can then identify a pattern of behavior that may have contributed to your persistent abuse of alcohol or drugs.

As presented in Principle Seven of the CSM, one of the most important concepts related to a more evolved understanding of addiction is the underrated value of spirituality. Over the years, I've seen countless people cast aside their addictions and embrace sobriety with the benefit of spiritual guidance.

Some clinicians and researchers feel that addiction is nothing more than a cry for help by those who feel spiritually unfulfilled. Dr Abraham Twerski agrees:

> *Most people learn through experience that certain substances provide a sense of gratification. Consequently, addictive thinking can lead people to try to quench this vague spiritual craving through food or drugs or sex or money. These objects*

may give some gratification, but they do nothing to solve the basic problem: the unmet spiritual needs.[58]

The idea that addicts are deliberately trying to destroy their own lives is ludicrous. They are simply people who don't know how to confront and cope with problems effectively. Substance abusers are guilty of one main failing—making self-destructive choices regarding drugs and alcohol. Most addicts are searching for spiritual answers, but they often settle for chemical solutions.

The AA concept of the "higher power" is a step in the right direction. This notion (although remarkably undefined) has been presented as a spiritual mechanism that helps addicts surrender control of their lives. When people find this concept useful, it can result in modifications in behavior that are clearly an improvement over the addiction, itself.

The Proven Benefits of Spirituality

More specifically, what role do religious beliefs play in an understanding of addiction? What does the current research reveal? Does it suggest any correlation between religion and sobriety? Gene Heyman offers the following answers:

> *Religious values typically teach self-restraint and sobriety. For those who endorse religious values, this settles the issue. They do not have to weigh either the short or long-term consequences of drug use. Rather, they have to decide whether or not they are religious or whether their religious proscriptions apply to the current situation. These turn out to be simpler decisions than whether or not to have a drink. Thus, the prediction is that differences in adherence to religious values are correlated with differences in drug use. The data support the predictions.*[59]

In other words, research affirms that people who embrace religious principles have lower rates of addictions. This is a monumental notion in the study of addiction theory. Simply put, religious people are less likely to be addicts than non-religious people. Gene Heyman concurs:

> *Those who prayed frequently and who endorsed the idea of a God who rewards and punishes reported lower levels of use or dependence on cigarettes and alcohol. The researchers' hunch that religion would play a role in times of stress was also confirmed. According to self-reports, stressful events typically increased smoking and drinking. But for those who strongly endorsed a belief in a spiritual world, there was no stress related increase in drug use.*[60]

Similar studies also found that adherence to traditional spiritual values and consistent church attendance were both associated with lower rates of addiction.[61]

The value of this information cannot be overstated. *Statistically speaking, religious beliefs give people a greater chance of beating or avoiding addiction, altogether.* But people aren't statistics—we are living, breathing, struggling human beings. Nevertheless, the data suggests that if addicts are able to wrap their minds around the concepts of religious enlightenment, they have a much greater chance of achieving permanent freedom from their addictions.

If you humbly examine your own behavior, you can begin to understand that you have placed yourself in the position of power. You have effectively chosen to worship at the "church of me." Dr. Abraham Twerski explains:

> *One feature of addictive thinking is the illusion of being in control. To some degree, a delusion of omnipotence (feeling one has unlimited power) is present in every addict. … The problem, however, isn't that the addict doesn't believe there is a God. Most believe deep down there is. The problem is they think they're God.*[62]

As human beings, we have done everything in our power to take control of our actions and emotions. We are undoubtedly in charge. The only problem is that when we grab the reigns and forsake God, wreckage is most often the result. Substance abuse can take a proud, positive person and turn them into a shell of their former self. The late psychiatrist Dr. Gerald May said it best,

> *Sooner or later, addiction will prove to us that we are not gods.*[63]

Conclusion

Obviously, addiction is not everything it has been made out to be. While it is undoubtedly dangerous and destructive, it most certainly is not a disease. Thinking back to our discussion on Dr. Jekyll and Mr. Hyde, I wonder about the theoretical consistencies involved. Mr. Hyde was a manifestation of each of Dr. Jekyll's negative emotions, and this was exhibited in his questionable conduct. But the malevolent characteristics displayed by Hyde were no doubt present within Dr. Jekyll before the experiment ever began. The potion did not cause his dark behavior; it just gave him the opportunity to put it on display.

What does this say about us? It confirms the fact that we are made up of both positive and negative elements in our character. The important thing to decide is which behaviors and emotions will dominate our lives. In this regard, I am no different than you, and you are no different than anyone else.

We do not suffer from the so-called disease of addiction. Famed addiction specialist Dr. William Playfair said it best:

> *Scripture tells us what alcohol and drug addiction is: sin. Thus, by implication it tells us what it is not: sickness.*[64]

PART II

Addiction, Sin, and Salvation

Do not gaze at wine when it is red, when it sparkles in the cup, when it goes down smoothly! In the end it bites like a snake and poisons like a viper. Your eyes will see strange sights, and your mind will imagine confusing things. You will be like one sleeping on the high seas, lying on top of the rigging. 'They hit me,' you will say, 'but I'm not hurt! They beat me, but I don't feel it! When will I wake up so I can find another drink?'

—Proverbs 23:31-35

CHAPTER TEN

Addictions and Sin: Two Peas in a Pod

Formerly, when you did not know God, you were slaves to those who by nature are not gods. But now that you know God—or rather are known by God—how is it that you are turning back to those weak and miserable principles? Do you wish to be enslaved by them all over again?

—The Apostle Paul
Galatians 4:8-9

B Y NOW IT should be clear that you are not a slave to chemicals, but a willing participant in your own addictive actions. As a result, your behavior must now be understood in the context of sin and not sickness. The problem is that most people prefer to be called sick rather than sinful. The simple change of a few letters takes all the pressure off. We can, therefore, blame a disease for our failings and justify our destructive behavior in the context of biology rather than choice. This is a predictably human response, but it does little to convince us that we have the capability to control our addictive behaviors.

We have been created by God with the ability to choose our own paths and by extension our own behaviors. The problem is that some of us have trouble moderating our behavior in the context of this unlimited freedom. We can't handle it, and we make mistakes. We need to learn to take charge of our behavior in order to avoid the pitfalls that accompany a lifestyle of substance abuse.

In our day-to-day lives, it is important to remember that sin and free will are partners in crime. Without the freedom of choice, you would lack the ability to sin. *Regardless of the opinions of others, you are not required to use drugs and alcohol. No one has a gun to your head, forcing you to take the next hit of heroin or chug the next beer. Our minds may want it, but our capacity for free will and choice have the veto power.*

There is one particular scripture that I feel describes addiction in its purest form. The Apostle Paul (whom we will discuss in later chapters) wrote the following words in the Bible's New Testament book of Romans. His writings are full of simple theological truths that get to the heart of the issues of morality and sin.

> *For I know that good itself does not dwell in me, that is, in my sinful nature. For I have the desire to do what is good, but I cannot carry it out.*
>
> **—Romans 7:18**

These words describe the phenomena of addiction in its most transparent form. Paul knows that he is flawed deep down to his core and that his life is built on a foundation of sin. He knows the difference between right and wrong and strives to do good things. Nevertheless, he has trouble turning his good intentions into good behavior. Sound familiar?

Since hallucinogenic narcotics are a relatively recent phenomena, the Bible speaks most often on the subject of addiction in terms of drinking and drunkenness. Alcohol was consumed with regularity in the ancient world, and drinking was not necessarily viewed as aberrant behavior. In fact, Jesus and his disciples drank wine every day, which shows us that drinking alcohol in moderation is not a sin.

However, a distinction must be made involving the overindulgence of wine and alcohol. Drinking as a concept was not frowned upon in the ancient world—just drinking to excess. The Apostle Paul wrote to the members of the church in Ephesus:

> *Therefore do not be foolish, but understand what the Lord's will is. Do not get drunk on wine, which leads to debauchery. Instead, be filled with the Spirit.*
>
> **—Ephesians 5:17-18**

Solomon, the son of King David, also wrote the following:

> *Wine is a mocker and beer a brawler; whoever is lead astray by them is not wise.*
>
> **—Proverbs 20:1**

These passages indicate that the problem with drinking (and by extension drugs) is primarily a problem of obedience and self-control.

What is Sin?

Before we can even think about avoiding sin, we should try to understand what it is. This question has plagued mankind for years, and it is one that is easily asked but not easily answered. Most contemporary dictionaries define "sin" as "the deliberate transgression of a religious or moral law."[65] This implies that the process of sinning breaks a law that has been established to guide the morally accepted aspects of a person's behavior. In other words, when you purposefully undertake any action that you know to be morally or religiously wrong, you have sinned.

The biblical definition of sin is a little different. The Hebrew and Greek words used in the original translation of the Old Testament for "sin" mean "to step across" or "to go beyond a set boundary."[66] In biblical terms, to commit sin means to willingly "step across" the line of acceptable behavior.

This definition implies within it an understanding of what is and is not considered acceptable behavior, which brings to mind the Ten Commandments. These ancient stone tablets, given to Moses in the Old Testament book of Exodus, detailed the ten major concepts for guiding acceptable behavior in the ancient world. Generally speaking, the first four commandments deal with man's relationship with God, including guidelines for worship and obedience. The final six commandments deal with man's relationships with others, such as the commands not to commit murder, theft, or adultery.

It is no coincidence that the very first commandment handed down by God involved putting Him first in our lives. This commandment, inscribed by the hand of God, is as follows:

> *You shall have no other gods before me.*
>
> **—Exodus 20:3**

The purpose of that statement was to confirm to the Israelites that they were to serve one … and only one God. This was a bold proclamation because most of the dominant cultures in antiquity promoted religions that worshiped multiple gods. In fact, the ancient Egyptians maintained the belief in a complex system of more than 60 gods.[67]

Addiction and Idolatry

In the Book of Exodus, God continued with a second commandment:

> *You shall not make for yourself an image in the form of anything in heaven above or on the earth beneath or in the waters below. You shall not bow down to them or worship them; for I, the Lord your God, am a jealous God …*
>
> **—Exodus 20:4-5**

This second commandment is all about the worship of physical objects and things other than God, himself. In biblical terms, this is known as idolatry. It is undoubtedly one of the greatest sins we can commit. Idolatry is all about love of self, which is the root cause of sin in all of our lives. Addiction Psychiatrist Dr. Gerald May concurs:

> *Spiritually, addiction is a deep-seated form of idolatry. The objects of our addictions become our false gods.*[68]

God does not require us to follow him; instead, He invites us to do so. Through the scriptures, He illuminates the divergent paths of obedience and disobedience in our lives. Although He discourages improper behavior, God's love is unconditional whether or not we decide to follow

His direction. Ultimately, we are granted the freedom to choose our own paths. Again, Dr. May states:

> *If our choice of God is to be made with integrity, we must first*
> *have felt other attractions and chosen, painfully, not to make*
> *them our gods. True love, then, is not only born of freedom;*
> *it is also born of difficult choice.*[69]

Essentially, we must learn to deny the voracious appetites of *self* in order to subdue our addictions. As humans, we most often worship at the *"church of me"* by spending all our time and effort desiring the things to which we assess the greatest value. We bow down to their power and influence, instead of turning control of our actions over to the Lord. Inevitably, our choices must be brought more into line with the will of God.

The Bible says we are all sinners as a result of having been born into this world. The actions of Adam and Eve (which we will discuss in the next chapter) sealed our fate in this regard. The Apostle Paul said it best:

> *... for all have sinned and fall short of the glory of God.*
> **—Romans 3:23**

The bottom line is that we often fail to recognize this simple fact. We all make mistakes, and addiction often tops the list. We are not necessarily diseased, but we suffer from a form of *soul sickness*. Having been born in sin, we must overcome the overwhelming urge to place our own desires in a position of prominence and power. We strive to be set free from the "slavery of sin," but we simply don't know how to do it.

As mentioned previously, spiritual help can be invaluable in attempting to conquer a persistent cycle of addiction. But in order to proceed, we must first examine the concepts of sin and sacrifice in the Bible. Once we've established a foundation of knowledge, we can then begin to understand the benefits of a life dedicated to following God. Jesus said the following:

> *Very truly I tell you, everyone who sins is a slave to sin. Now a*
> *slave has no permanent place in the family, but a son belongs*
> *to it forever. So if the Son sets you free, you will be free indeed.*
> **—John 8:34-36**

The year was 1987 and I was preparing to begin my freshman year at Syracuse University. I remember the excitement of embarking on an new chapter in my life, but having to do so without my little brother and best friend. When I left home that fall, I felt the anxiety of separation in a very sharp and powerful way. But I never anticipated the events that would follow ... even in my worst nightmares.

Evidently, Kevin's substance abuse began at the tender age of 15. It started innocently enough as he began smoking marijuana with his friends. He liked it fairly well, but he eventually craved a more potent high. In the years that followed, he would work his way down the diabolical path from marijuana to cocaine and eventually to heroin. Like most substance abusers, he was a gifted liar and kept most of his activities hidden behind a veil of innocence and ignorance.

His addiction eventually got so bad that he would disappear for months at a time, leaving our family to wonder if he was even still alive. As his substance abuse escalated, he lived on the streets, sold drugs for profit, and got an up close and personal view of hell on earth. Kevin was shot at and stabbed, and he spent many cold winter nights in garbage dumpsters. One time he even had the barrel of a .45 caliber revolver shoved into his mouth. Despite the dangers, he managed to survive all these encounters with the help of what he called "the protection of the hand of God." He knew God had gotten him out of some life threatening situations, but he really didn't understand why. Nor could he fathom the unconditional love of our family as we embraced him with non-condemning acceptance upon his return.

Over the years, a pattern of rehabilitation, periods of non-active use, and relapse ensued. When he jumped back into the fray again, he would do anything in his power to prolong his drug habit. Since his upbringing was of the highest quality, he admittedly denied that he had any reason to "escape" from his family life. He simply cared about getting "high" more than he cared about anything else.

CHAPTER ELEVEN

God and Sacrifice in the Old Testament

The fool says in his heart, 'There is no God.'
—King David
Psalm 53:1

T HE FIRST FIVE books of the Bible were written by Moses and other unnamed authors sometime around 1500 BC. They contain the majority of the historical accounts of the Old Testament and serve as a theological backdrop for later writings. In order to understand the concept of sin and sacrifice in the Old Testament, we will begin with a brief overview of the text.

In the very first chapter of the Book of Genesis, God created the heavens and the earth. He then created all the plants and animals on the land and in the sea. He finished his work on the sixth day with the creation of mankind. On the seventh day, God looked over his creation and rested, introducing the concept of the Sabbath (which means "to rest from labor").

So God created man in his own image, in the image of God he created him; male and female he created them."
—Genesis 1:27

The first man Adam and his companion Eve were placed in the Garden of Eden. They lived in harmony with God's creation in the Garden, and all of their needs were met. They were told they could eat fruit from any tree or plant in the garden, with the exception of "the tree of knowledge of good and evil." If they disobeyed God's command and ate from this particular tree, they would "surely die."

In the midst of this idyllic environment, Eve was tempted by a serpent (a symbol of the devil) to question God's instructions. The serpent refuted the claim that eating from this tree would result in death. Instead, he told her that she would become "like" God, knowing good and evil. When Eve saw that the fruit was pleasing to the eye, she ate it and shared it with Adam. Afterwords, they were overwhelmed with shame and fear. They recognized their nakedness and tried to hide in the Garden from their Creator.

God responded to their disobedience by forcing them to labor to provide for their own existence. Also, these formerly immortal beings would experience death. They were banished from the garden, and God placed angels and a flaming sword to guard the entrance and further access to the "tree of life."

This act of rebellion against God marked the entrance of sin into the world. These actions signaled the beginning of the endless human cycle of loving self over loving God. By choosing to eat the fruit, Adam and Eve put their own desires above those of God. This biblical story of *original sin* has become widely known as the "fall of man."

Over the next several hundred years, the prevalence of sin increased. Eventually, man's sinful nature became so distasteful to God that He could find only a few people on the earth who continued to follow Him. As a result, He decided to cleanse the earth of sin by way of a massive flood, choosing only to save a faithful man named Noah and his family. Noah dutifully obeyed God's command to build an ark to save his family as well as every species of animal that had been created.

Abraham to the Exodus

As a sign of God's mercy in judgment, the earth became repopulated after the flood. Likewise, sin gained influence in the following several hundred years. People again became engrossed in their own lives and failed to follow God. Because of man's ignorance and his obsession with sin, God turned his attention to the task of redeeming mankind as a whole. To do so, God revealed himself to an honorable man named Abram (later known as Abraham), who would become the father of the Hebrew people. God made a covenant with Abraham, promising him blessings and generations of descendants in exchange for faithfulness and obedience. Abraham was led into a land known as Canaan where he settled with his wife and children.

The promises of God were then passed down through Isaac, one of Abraham's sons. Isaac was a godly man and continued the family line. God's covenant was once again passed down through Isaac's son Jacob, and his descendants thrived in the sight of God. Although Jacob was by no means perfect, he succeeded despite his many faults. Jacob fathered a dozen sons, who would basically become the patriarchs of the original twelve tribes of Israel.

Jacob's family prospered in the land of Canaan and their numbers increased. They later migrated to Egypt to escape a vicious famine that had befallen their land. They settled in Egypt where food was available and remained there for many years. As the Hebrews increased in number, they began to be perceived as a military threat by the Egyptians. In order to avoid this potential problem, the Egyptians decided to oppress and enslave the Hebrew people.

Under the authority of the Egyptian Pharoah, the Hebrew people were exploited and abused for more than 400 years. Eventually, God decided to intervene on their behalf. He called a man named Moses (a Hebrew, who had been found and raised by Pharoah's sister) to bring about the Hebrew's release from slavery. After God tormented the Egyptians with numerous plagues, the Lord's "chosen people" were released from service and the Exodus began. Moses led between two and three million Hebrews out of Egypt into the Sinai Desert.

After Pharoah granted freedom to God's people, he had a change of heart and sent out his army to destroy them. As the Hebrews fled from Pharoah's army, they became trapped between the approaching soldiers and the Red Sea. In order to preserve his people, God parted the Red Sea, allowing the Hebrews to cross safely on dry land. After they reached the other side, Pharoah's army was destroyed as the walls of water collapsed and overwhelmed them. Under Moses' leadership, the people then traveled across the desert to Mt. Sinai where God gave them the Ten Commandments.

In fulfillment of His word, God led His people to a place called Kadesh Barnea, which was on the edge of Canaan (the Hebrew's Promised Land). Despite witnessing the power of God during their exodus from Egypt, the people were overcome with fear and doubted their ability to conquer the people of that land. Due to their lack of faith, God banished them to wander aimlessly in the desert wilderness for forty years.

Once the generation of the unfaithful died out, God chose Joshua to take His people across the Jordan River in a campaign to conquer the Promised Land. God parted the Jordan River as the Israelites carried the Ark of the Covenant (which held the original tablets of the Ten Commandments) into Canaan. With divine assistance from the Lord, Joshua led the people to victory over the inhabitants of the land.

Having conquered Canaan, the Israelites settled in the Promised Land. For the first 400 years or so, Israel was ruled by a loose system of regional leaders called Judges. Rulers like Samson and Samuel led the loosely held nation in this turbulent period. Around 1000 BC, rather than resting in the authority of God, the Israelites insisted on installing a monarchy to rule their land. A man named Saul was chosen as the first king of the nation of Israel, which consisted of descendants from the twelve original tribes. His tumultuous rule was marred by dissension and the kingdom eventually divided.

King David and Sacrifice in the Temple

Since Saul disobeyed the direct commands of the Lord, he was replaced by a man of God's choosing. David (a former shepherd boy) rose to fame as the youngster who engaged in solitary combat with Goliath, a Philistine warrior. In this story, the Israelite and Philistine armies were poised for battle on either side of the Valley of Elah. Rather than have the armies meet in a full scale battle, the giant Goliath challenged the Israelites to send out a single man to fight him. The victor of this engagement (which was not uncommon in ancient times) would decide the outcome of the war. However, none of Israel's soldiers were courageous enough to answer Goliath's challenge. Although David was merely a boy and not a soldier in Saul's army, he showed complete faith in God's power by responding to Goliath's arrogant summons and slaying him with a single smooth stone from his slingshot.

David matured into a mighty warrior and gained favor with the people of God. King David was chosen by God to reunite the twelve tribes into the United Kingdom era. Although David was undoubtedly a godly man, he was far from perfect. Nevertheless, David was a righteous king and ruled justly in Israel for many years.

King David wanted to honor God by building a temple in Jerusalem in which to house the Ark of the Covenant. Since David was a man of war, God would not allow him to build the temple in Jerusalem. Instead he would prepare for its construction and plan much of its administration and worship services. Even though David was denied the privilege of building the temple, God promised to allow his descendants to occupy the throne of Israel forever.

The building of the temple (which symbolized the dwelling place of God) would be accomplished by David's son, Solomon. In only seven years, Solomon built God's temple in Jerusalem into one of the most exquisite buildings in antiquity. The temple, which had inner and outer courts, housed the Ark of the Covenant in an extraordinary chamber known as the "Holy of Holies." Once a year, the Chief Priest would enter this inner sanctum to burn incense and pray.

The entire Old Testament sacrificial system (outlined by Moses in the Book of Leviticus) was undertaken at God's temple in Jerusalem. The people of Israel were required to atone for their sins by offering gifts and animal sacrifices at the temple. They would bring lambs, for instance, and present them to the Levite priests at the temple to be sacrificed to God on their behalf. Pouring the animal's blood on the altar was the mechanism by which the entire nation of Israel received forgiveness for their sins.

Once a year on the Day of Atonement, the High Priest would first sacrifice a bull as an offering to God for his personal sins. He would then present two goats at the door of the temple with the intent of addressing the corporal sins of the people. One goat would be designated as "The Lord's Goat" and offered within the temple as a blood sacrifice. The blood of this slain goat would be sprinkled directly on the "mercy seat," otherwise known as the lid of the Ark of the Covenant. The other goat, known as the "Azazel" goat, would be figuratively burdened with the sins of all Israel and released into the wilderness, never to return. This symbolic practice, undertaken one day each year, gave rise to the modern term "scapegoat."

After Solomon's death, the nation of Israel once again became divided. In 930 BC, ten of the original twelve tribes broke away from the rest and came together to form the Northern Kingdom of Israel. The remaining tribes joined forces in the south to become the Southern Kingdom of Judah, named for its largest original tribe. This division of the tribes weakened the kingdoms and made them attractive targets for conquest by other nations.

The Exile, the Return, and the Romans

In the years following Solomon's reign, the sin of idolatry spread like a disease in the nation of Israel. Many towns and cities built temples to worship pagan gods, leading the people away from worshiping the one true God. As a result of this disloyalty and sin, God allowed the nation of Assyria to conquer the Northern Kingdom of Israel in 722 BC and scatter its inhabitants. For similar reasons, God allowed the nation of Babylon to capture and destroy the Southern Kingdom of Judah about 150 years later. The temple and all of Jerusalem was destroyed in the process, while many of its inhabitants were taken into exile in Babylon.

During the exile, numerous prophets (such as Ezekiel and Daniel) began to predict the resurgence of Israel and the rebuilding of the temple in Jerusalem. In the meantime, the Persian Empire rose to prominence and defeated the Babylonians, who had previously defeated the Assyrians. Prompted by God, the Persian King Cyrus then allowed the Jews (a name derived from a description of the people from the tribe of Judah) to return to their homeland. The prophet Nehemiah and about fifty thousand others returned to the Holy Land and started resurrecting the city and the nation itself. The walls around Jerusalem were rebuilt, and a second temple was constructed around 500 BC.

In the centuries that followed, the influence of the Persians faded and gave way to the rise of the Roman Empire. The Roman general Pompey conquered the Land of Israel in 63 BC, thereafter referring to the region as "Palestine." The Romans, having no interest in stirring rebellion among the natives, allowed a Hebrew named Herod the Great to control Palestine under the watchful supervision of a Roman administrator. The Jews were allowed to continue practicing their native religion and maintain the Levitical sacrificial system at the temple in Jerusalem.

Before the conquest of the Northern and Southern Kingdoms, God appointed a few specific followers as prophets to communicate His wishes to the people. Famous men such as Isaiah and Jeremiah foretold the destruction of the temple and the nation itself. During those turbulent years, the people began hoping for a new leader to rise up and fulfill the role of Messiah (which means "deliverer"). Because of the militant nature of their history, most Jews expected God to send them a zealous, military style leader to expel the foreigners and usher in a new kingdom ordained by God.

Old Testament Messianic Prophecy

There are about 60 different Old Testament prophecies related to the coming of the Messiah. The first of these prophecies was probably written as many as 400 years before the birth of Jesus with the last one no less than 200 years prior. The Book of Isaiah includes some of the most famous and recognizable verses of messianic prophecy. For instance, Isaiah wrote:

> *Therefore the Lord himself will give you a sign. The virgin will conceive and give birth to a son, and will call him Immanuel (God with us).*
>
> **—Isaiah 7:14**

He continued along those lines two chapters later:

> *For to us a child is born, to us a son is given, and the government will be on his shoulders. And he will be called Wonderful Counselor, Mighty God, Everlasting Father, Prince of Peace.*
>
> **—Isaiah 9:6**

Isaiah painted the picture of a Messiah to come that would be born of a virgin mother and be the physical incarnation of God. These two pieces of scripture are fairly consistent with the prevailing view of the Messiah at the time of the Babylonian captivity. His message was primarily intended to give hope to those Jews in exile that God's holy kingdom would endure.

The following prophecy, however, is a bit of a departure from the traditional messianic thinking and points us more toward the idea of a more pacifistic "deliverer" to come.

> *But he was pierced for our transgressions, he was crushed for our iniquities; the punishment that brought us peace was on him, and by his wounds we are healed. … Therefore, I will give him a portion among the great, and he will divide the spoils with the strong, because he poured out his life unto death, and was outnumbered with the transgressors. For he bore the sin of many and made intercession for the transgressors.*
>
> **—Isaiah 53:5-12**

In these scriptures, we are introduced to the idea of a Messiah who intercedes for us between the manifestation of our sins and God. As stated earlier, the Old Testament concept of atonement for sin involved a complicated system of gifts and animal sacrifices made in regularity to atone for inappropriate behavior. The blood of a sacrifice was literally sprinkled on the temple altar for the forgiveness of sins.

Isaiah presented one of the first hints that the coming Messiah would satisfy the traditional requirements of the sacrificial instrument by which all would be redeemed. Those writings, likely completed hundreds of years before the birth of Jesus, pointed in the direction of a new blood covenant that would be offered for the forgiveness of sins.

At the time of creation, Adam and Eve had chosen self will over God's will. They were punished for their actions by their banishment from the Garden of Eden. In this way, sin emerged as a powerful force in the lives of all mankind. Consequently, we are all "born" into sin, carrying the burden of the actions of Adam and Eve as a weight which is heavy to bear. We are, therefore, condemned as sinners from conception and are in need of redemption from the time we take our first breath. The Apostle Paul agreed:

> *Therefore, just as sin entered the world through one man, and death through sin, and in this way death came to all people, because all sinned...*
>
> **—Romans 5:12**

God understands the gravity of our relationship with sin. Addictions, like all other sins, have been thrust upon us at conception. Not surprisingly, we then struggle on a daily basis to balance the weight of our sins with the will of our God. While we may be unsuccessful for the most part, we have not been assigned the task of conquering our sinful desires alone. Indeed, the much prophesied Messiah would walk the earth hundreds of years later in the form of a man, born of a virgin in an ancient place called Bethlehem.

CHAPTER TWELVE

Jesus Becomes Our Sacrifice in the New Testament

I am the resurrection and the life. The one who believes in me will live, even though they die; and whoever lives by believing in me will never die. Do you believe this?

—Jesus of Nazareth
John 11:25-26

THE ROMAN GENERAL Pompey conquered the Holy Land in 63 BC and took control of the city of Jerusalem. In the process, the Romans massacred priests and defiled the temple, stirring animosity among the occupied Jews. Despite their brutality, the Romans attempted to appease the Orthodox sensibilities of the people and avoid rebellion by allowing the continued practice of temple worship in Jerusalem. While their own religion was based on the belief in many different gods, the Romans recognized the importance of maintaining the traditional religious practices of the Jews. Despite being allowed to worship in accordance with their beliefs, the Jews longed for the promised Messiah to liberate them from the burdens of Roman authority.

The Birth Story

The birth of the prophesied Messiah was proclaimed by the angel Gabriel to a peasant woman named Mary. She had been pledged in marriage to a righteous man named Joseph (a carpenter from Nazareth) who was a direct descendant of King David. In the visitation, Mary was informed that she would conceive a child through the workings of the Holy Spirit. Upon learning of Mary's pregnancy, Joseph decided to divorce her quietly in order to spare her from public disgrace. Note: According to ancient custom, once a couple became engaged, it would take a decree of divorce to end the relationship (even before an actual marriage ceremony took place). Before Joseph took action, an angel of the Lord appeared to him in a dream and told him not to be concerned about proceeding with the marriage:

> *… what is conceived in her (Mary) is from the Holy Spirit.*
> *She will give birth to a son, and you are to give him the name*
> *Jesus, because he will save his people from their sins.*
> **—Matthew 1:20-21**

As the result of a decree from the Roman emperor Caesar Augustus, all citizens of Palestine were to return to the town of their ancestral origin to participate in a census. Therefore, Mary and Joseph traveled to the town of Bethlehem, which was not far from Jerusalem. Soon after their arrival, Mary gave birth to a child and named him "Jesus" as instructed. The actual birth likely took place in a cave or animal pen. Jesus' birth and the declaration of his messiahship were heralded by angels to local shepherds in the field.

> *And there were shepherds living out in the fields nearby,*
> *keeping watch over their flocks at night. An angel of the Lord*
> *appeared to them, and the glory of the Lord shone around*
> *them, and they were terrified. But the angel said to them, 'Do*
> *not be afraid. I bring you good news that will cause great joy*
> *for all the people. Today in the town of David a Savior has*
> *been born you; he is the Messiah, the Lord.'*
> **—Luke 2:8-11**

The name Jesus is an English translation of the Hebrew name "Joshua" (pronounced Ye-shu-a). It is derived from the Hebrew word that means "savior." The term "Christ" is not a name; it is actually a title. The English word "Christ" comes from the Greek word "christos," which means "Messiah." So Jesus Christ is actually presented more correctly as "Yeshua the Messiah."

Jesus' Early Life and Ministry

According to custom, Mary and Joseph took Jesus to the temple shortly after his birth to present him before the Lord. When they arrived at the temple, they were met by a devout Jew named Simeon. God had revealed to Simeon that he would not die before having looked upon the Lord's Messiah. Upon seeing Jesus, Simeon proclaimed:

> *Sovereign Lord, as you have promised, you may now dismiss your servant in peace. For my eyes have seen your salvation, which you have prepared in the sight of all nations: a light for revelation to the Gentiles (non-Jews) and for glory to your people Israel.*
>
> **—Luke 2:29-32**

This event establishes the early divinity of Jesus, even before he was old enough to speak. Other than the fact that he was raised in a godly home and learned to work with his hands, not much else is known about his childhood.

At the time, a relative of Jesus known as John the Baptist was spending a great deal of time in the Jordan Valley preaching baptism (ritual immersion) for the forgiveness of sins. John's birth had also been foretold, when an angel of the Lord proclaimed that he would "prepare the way" for the coming of the Messiah.

Around 30 AD, Jesus traveled to the shores of the Jordan River to be baptized by his cousin John. At first, John protested this arrangement on the grounds that he was not worthy to baptize Jesus, whom he immediately recognized as the Messiah. Nevertheless, Jesus stepped into the waters of the Jordan and was baptized in the name of the Lord. Luke described the scene:

When all the people were being baptized, Jesus was baptized too. And as he was praying, heaven was opened and the Holy Spirit descended on him in bodily form like a dove. And a voice came from heaven: 'You are my Son, whom I love; with you I am well pleased.'

—Luke 4:21-22

The voice from heaven belonged to God, identifying Jesus as the much prophesied Messiah. John the Baptist confirmed this notion:

And I myself did not know him, but the one who sent me to baptize with water told me, 'The man on whom you see the Spirit come down and remain is he who will baptize with the Holy Spirit.' I have seen and I testify that this is the Son of God.

—John 1:33-34

Immediately following his baptism, Jesus withdrew into the wilderness. In the midst of forty days of fasting and praying, he was tempted by the Devil, himself. Jesus rebuked Satan with scripture three times, and emerged victorious to begin the task of spreading the gospel (which means "good news") about the kingdom of God.

As his public ministry began, Jesus met fishermen brothers named Peter and Andrew near the Sea of Galilee. They were the first of the original disciples to be chosen.

'Come follow me,' Jesus said, 'and I will make you fishers of men.'

—Matthew 4:19

Jesus continued to travel throughout Palestine, gaining many followers in the process. He issued his much acclaimed Sermon on the Mount (as described in the Gospel of Matthew) to thousands of onlookers near Capernaum on the Sea of Galilee. He is portrayed in this text in comparison to Moses, standing on a hillside proclaiming the principles of righteous living through God.

Jesus was not just a dynamic speaker. He was also appointed by God to conduct miracles, ranging from simple healings to raising people from the dead. He fed 5,000 followers with a handful of bread and fish, calmed a fierce storm on the Sea of Galilee, and cast out demons in the name of God the Father. These miracles served to establish his divinity and authority to the people of the time. On the subject of miracles, Jesus stated the following:

> *Believe me when I say that I am in the Father and the Father is in me; or at least believe on the evidence of the works themselves.*
>
> **—John 14:11**

One of the key teachings of Jesus' earthly ministry lies within the following passage:

> *'Love the Lord your God with all your heart and with all your soul and with all your mind. This is the first and greatest commandment. And the second is like it: Love your neighbor as yourself. All the Law and the Prophets hang on these two commandments.'*
>
> **—Matthew 22:37-40**

In this case, Jesus went about simplifying the original Ten Commandments by breaking them down into two basic principles. Jesus stated that to love God and to love others are the two most important commandments. All the remaining principles of godly living are built upon the foundation of these two divine laws.

As his ministry flourished, many people began to refer to Jesus as the "Son of David" or the "Son of Man"—both of which are Old Testament references to the Messiah. In fact, Jesus openly accepted this title in an encounter with a Samaritan woman. Remember—the Samaritans and the Jews had great disdain for one another, going back to the Old Testament division of the Northern and Southern Kingdoms. The following is a portion of the conversation between this woman and Jesus regarding his messiahship:

> *The woman said, 'I know that Messiah (called Christ) is coming. When he comes, he will explain everything to us.' Then Jesus declared, 'I, the one speaking to you- I am he.'*
> **—John 4:25-26**

This startling admission to a Samaritan woman was significant because Jews did not normally associate with Samaritans.

So instead of avoiding the title of Messiah, Jesus settled the question altogether by embracing it. In the midst of the Roman occupation of Palestine, this was a very dangerous move to make. Don't forget that the Jews were waiting for a militant, rebellious figure to rise up as Messiah and end the horrors of the Roman occupation. In his public declaration as Messiah, Jesus was risking his very life. Nevertheless, he wholeheartedly embraced his position as God's divine "deliverer." He stated clearly:

> *I and the Father are one.*
> **—John 10:30**

Jesus Becomes the Sacrifice

While Jesus was unambiguous in his claims, he also understood that his life was to be offered as a sacrifice for the sins of mankind. Jesus stated that fact quite clearly:

> *For even the Son of Man did not come to be served but to serve, and to give his life as a ransom for many.*
> **—Mark 10:45**

He understood that his life would be surrendered so that the Old Testament sacrificial system might be discontinued and fulfilled in his being.

The apostles eventually began to understand the true nature of his divinity. In fact, Jesus asked his disciples to state plainly who they believed him to be. Peter, a leader among the disciples, answered without hesitation:

You are the Messiah, the Son of the living God.
—Matthew 16:16

The Gospels make the crystalline case that Jesus was the Son of God. He willingly sacrificed his life to offer atonement for the sins of all of mankind. Instead of continuing the ritual practice of animal sacrifices at the temple, believers need only to accept the one-time final sacrifice of Jesus for the redemption of their sins. Jesus confirmed this fact in his own words:

> *The reason my Father loves me is that I lay down my life— only to take it up again. No one takes it from me, but I lay it down of my own accord. … This command I received from my Father.*
>
> **—John 10:17-18**

As Jesus continued to travel and teach, he began to prophesy about the nature of things yet to come. He understood his role in a larger sense and relayed the gravity of coming events to his followers in simple terms:

> *The Son of Man must be delivered over to the hands of sinners, be crucified and on the third day raised again.*
>
> **—Luke 24:7**

The disciples stubbornly refused to believe these words and struggled to comprehend the full impact of the events that were about to unfold.

Jerusalem at Passover

In the third and final year of his public ministry, Jesus and his disciples traveled to Jerusalem to celebrate Passover. In an event that has become known as Palm Sunday, Jesus arrived in Jerusalem on the back of a donkey colt. The details of this event had been foretold 500 years earlier by the Old Testament prophet Zechariah. Many of Jesus' followers met him at the gates of the city and laid palm leaves in his path to announce his arrival as the Messiah. This event stunned the Jewish authorities, because this practice was primarily reserved for welcoming royalty in antiquity.

Once inside the city, Jesus made his way to the temple. There he drove out the moneylenders and the merchants selling animals for sacrifices. Luke described the scene:

> *When Jesus entered the temple courts, he began to drive out those who were selling. 'It is written,' he said to them, 'My house will be a house of prayer but you have made it a den of robbers.' Every day he was teaching at the temple. But the chief priests, the teachers of the law and the leaders among the people were trying to kill him.*
>
> **—Luke 19:45-47**

These events raised the profile of Jesus in the minds of the Jewish elite and their Roman occupiers. The Jewish priestly power base feared the popularity of Jesus, and had been plotting behind the scenes to discredit him for some time. They viewed him as a direct threat to their spiritual and financial control of the lives of the people. They feared that his emerging popularity might lead to the total collapse of institutional worship at the temple. The Jewish High Priest, a man named Caiaphas, would stop at nothing to maintain control of his position in the religious and social hierarchy in Jerusalem. He was quoted in the Gospel of John as saying the following:

> *You do not realize that it is better for you that one man die for the people than that the whole nation perish.*
>
> **—John 11:50**

The temple priests and the Pharisees (an influential group of self-righteous law givers) feared that a rise in the popularity of Jesus would affect their relative positions in the sociopolitical realm of the day. They wanted to destroy Jesus and fractionalize his following in order to preserve their own positions of power.

As the week unfolded, Jesus told his disciples to prepare a Passover meal in an "upper room" inside the city. This special feast was celebrated annually to commemorate the night (prior to the Exodus) on which the angel of death "passed over" the homes of the Hebrew slaves, taking only the lives of the firstborn children of Egypt. At this gathering, Jesus performed the ritual known as the Last Supper.

> *And he took bread, gave thanks and broke it, and gave it*
> *to them, saying, 'This is my body given for you; do this in*
> *remembrance of me.' In the same way after the supper he took*
> *the cup, saying, 'This cup is the new covenant in my blood,*
> *which is poured out for you.'*
>
> **—Luke 22:19-20**

Jesus chose that occasion to reveal the specific nature of the events to come. He boldly stated that one of the twelve disciples in attendance would betray him. The identity of this person was known to Jesus but unknown to the remaining eleven faithful disciples. Jesus told Judas Iscariot (the betrayer) to "do quickly" what he must do. Judas then exited the feast to deliver Jesus into the hands of the Jewish authorities for thirty pieces of silver.

The Arrest and Crucifixion

After the meal, Jesus and the remaining disciples made their way to the Garden of Gethsemane on the outskirts of Jerusalem. By that time, darkness had fallen and Jesus went off alone to pray.

> *He withdrew about a stone's throw beyond them, knelt down*
> *and prayed, 'Father, if you are willing, take this cup from*
> *me; yet not my will, but yours be done.' An angel from heaven*
> *appeared to him and strengthened him. And being in anguish*
> *he prayed more earnestly, and his sweat was like drops of*
> *blood falling to the ground.*
>
> **—Luke 22:41-43**

Shortly thereafter, a large crowd of men appeared looking for the holy man from Nazareth. Judas identified Jesus among the other disciples by kissing him on the cheek. The chief priests and guards from the temple arrested Jesus and took him before a group known as the Sanhedrin. This organization (which was made up of around seventy priests, scribes, and Pharisees) served as the judicial court that interpreted and guarded Jewish laws. At that trial, which took place that same evening, the high priest interrogated Jesus and accused him of blasphemy against God. The Gospel of Mark describes one particular exchange:

> *Again the high priest asked him, 'Are you the Messiah, the*
> *Son of the Blessed One?' 'I am,' said Jesus. 'And you will see*
> *the Son of Man sitting at the right hand of the Mighty One*
> *and coming on the clouds of heaven.'*
> **—Mark 14:61-62**

The Jewish accusers were enraged by these words and reacted swiftly in proclaiming his guilt. Jesus was beaten and taken for sentencing before the ruling Roman governor of Palestine. This man named Pontius Pilate had developed a well-deserved reputation for cruelty across the land. However in this case, Pilate did not find Jesus to be guilty of any crime worthy of death. In fact, he tried to release Jesus to the crowd which had assembled before him. (Note: During the Passover celebration, it was customary for the Romans to release one prisoner as a gesture of goodwill to the Jews.) When he offered to release Jesus, the crowd was incited by supporters of the Jewish elite to demand the release of another prisoner. They then emphatically called for Jesus to be executed. Pontius Pilate acquiesced, sentencing Jesus to die by crucifixion.

Jesus was then viciously flogged by his Roman captors. The Romans used a whip called a *flagrum*, which was made of leather into which they embedded pieces of bone or lead. Floggings overseen by the Romans involved thirty-nine or more blows with this whip, and many victims of this abuse did not survive the beatings. Jesus, however, endured the blows and was taken into the palace to be prepared for execution. The guards beat him, mocking him as the so-called "King of the Jews." They placed a crown of thorns on his head and led him out to be crucified.

Roman crucifixion was a popular means of torture and execution, generally reserved for criminals who had committed capital offenses. The condemned were most often nailed to a cross with six inch iron spikes through their wrists and ankles. Victims of this punishment would hang from a cross until they were unable to bear their own body weight, thereby dying of asphyxiation. In fact, death by crucifixion was considered so brutal that a word was created to describe it. The term *excruciating* (which literally means "out of the cross") comes from this brutal ancient practice. Crucifixion was considered by Jewish law to be the most dishonorable death imaginable.

Jesus was nailed to the cross at around nine o'clock in the morning. He was crucified alongside two criminals on a hill called Golgotha, which means the "place of the skull." The Bible says that darkness fell on the land around noon and the sun stopped shining for a while. After a few hours on the cross, Jesus succumbed:

> *Later, knowing that everything had now been finished and so that scripture would be fulfilled … Jesus said, 'It is finished,' With that he bowed his head and gave up his spirit.*
> **—John 19:28-30**

Jesus died a physical death on the cross around three o'clock in the afternoon. To confirm his death, a Roman soldier pierced his side with a spear, bringing forth a sudden flow of blood and water. His mother Mary and others witnessed his passing and helped to take his body down from the cross. A rich man named Joseph of Arimathea (who was a member of the Sanhedrin and a secret follower of Jesus) offered the tomb in which Jesus' remains were interred. In order to obey God's commandment of honoring the Sabbath, it was necessary to wrap his body in a linen cloth and seal it in the tomb before sundown.

The Resurrection and Ascension

On the morning of the third day, the women returned to the tomb with the intention of preparing Jesus' body for final burial. They planned to anoint the body with spices and perfumes in accordance with Jewish burial customs. When they arrived, they were astonished by what they saw. Luke described the scene:

*They found the stone rolled away from the tomb, but when
they entered, they did not find the body of the Lord Jesus.
While they were wondering about this, suddenly two men
in clothes that gleamed like lightning stood beside them.
In their fright the women bowed down with their faces to
the ground, but the men said to them, 'Why do you look
for the living among the dead? He (Jesus) is not here; he
has risen!'*

—Luke 24:2-6

The two men in the tomb were angels, and they announced that Jesus
had been resurrected. Understandably excited, the women ran back to tell
the remaining disciples what they had seen. Peter and the others raced to
the tomb to verify these claims for themselves. Indeed, the tomb was empty
and the body of Jesus was nowhere to be found.

In the days following his crucifixion, Jesus made about a dozen post-
resurrection appearances. One such event is described in the Gospel of
John where Jesus appeared to nearly all of his disciples a short time after
his resurrection. Luke writes:

*On the evening of the first day of the week, when the
disciples were together, with the doors locked for fear of the
Jewish leaders, Jesus came and stood among them and said,
'Peace be with you!' After he said this, he showed them his
hands and side. The disciples were overjoyed when they saw
the Lord.*

—Luke 20:19-20

One of the disciples named Thomas was not in attendance. Upon
his return, he stubbornly refused to believe that his companions had
really seen Christ. Thomas declared that until he could see and touch
the resurrected Jesus for himself, he would not believe. A few days later,
Thomas was given the following opportunity:

*A week later his disciples were in the house again, and
Thomas was with them. Though the doors were locked, Jesus*

came and stood among them and said, 'Peace be with you!'
Then he said to Thomas, 'Put your finger here; see my hands.
Reach out your hand and put it into my side. Stop doubting
and believe.'

—John 20:26-27

Thomas saw Jesus in his post-resurrected body with the nail and spear marks still visible. Having done so, Thomas fell on his face and worshiped him as the risen Messiah. This story gave rise to the modern description of a skeptical person as a "doubting Thomas."

Jesus gave his disciples specific instructions before he ascended to heaven. Matthew wrote:

Then Jesus came to them and said, 'All authority in heaven
and on earth has been given to me. Therefore go and make
disciples of all nations, baptizing them in the name of the
Father and of the Son and of the Holy Spirit, and teaching
them to obey everything I have commanded you. And surely
I am with you always, to the very end of the age.'

—Matthew 28:18-20

He then led them into a village known as Bethany, where he blessed them and was taken up into heaven.

CHAPTER THIRTEEN

Will the Real Messiah Please Stand Up!

The Word (Jesus) became flesh and made his dwelling among us. We have seen his glory, the glory of the One and Only, who came from the Father, full of grace and truth.
—John 1:14

HAVING DISCUSSED THE significant events that took place in the life of Jesus, we are faced with some interesting questions. For instance, what evidence do we have that Jesus actually lived? How confident are we that the accounts written in the Gospels are accurate? And finally, how can we be sure that Jesus was really the Messiah? Let's deal with these questions one at a time.

How do we know for certain that Jesus of Nazareth actually existed? Interestingly, one answer to this question lies in the details concerning the authors of the Gospels that tell his story. Of the four Gospels presented in the New Testament, two were written by actual eyewitnesses of the events they described.

The Gospel of Matthew was written by a former tax collector who left his job to follow Jesus. This man (also known in the scriptures as the "son of Alphaeus") is undeniably the same disciple called Matthew described in Chapter 9 of the first Gospel. Additionally, the Gospel of John was written by another disciple of Jesus known as "John, son of Zebedee." So both Matthew and John were actual eyewitnesses of the events that transpired.

They wrote their accounts relying on nothing more than their own memories of the stories as they happened. They witnessed many of the miracles being performed, and they both saw Jesus in his post-resurrection body.

The remaining two Gospels were written by close companions of famous disciples. The author of the Gospel of Mark was a close companion of the Apostle Peter. Luke (who wrote the gospel that bears his name) was a close companion of the Apostle Paul. Both Peter and Paul had personal experiences with Jesus, and together their writings account for more than 70% of the material in the New Testament. Therefore, Mark and Luke wrote their gospels based on information provided directly to them by two of the most influential Christians leaders in the history of the early church.

The Supporting Evidence

As of today, there are about 24,000 copies of New Testament manuscripts from ancient times in existence. That's a very large number, considering that many of these copies were produced more than 19 centuries ago. Additionally, the New Testament has survived in a purer form than any other great book from history. The existing copies examined by scholars are said to be 99.5% similar in terms of content.[70] In other words, all of the copies of the New Testament that have been discovered over the years are within half a percent of being identical.

In addition, corroborating third party evidence exists for the life and impact of Christ in many other sources from antiquity. Jesus is mentioned in the Talmud, a Jewish rabbinical text that emerged around 200 AD. A Roman senator named Tacitus also spoke of Jesus in his major writings about the reigns of such Roman Emperors as Claudius and Nero. Another Roman writer known as Pliny included evidence about Jesus in his many writings. He and his works were well-known in antiquity, as he was actually the governor of ancient Bithynia in Northern Turkey. Finally, the famous Jewish historian Flavius Josephus wrote the following in his first century work entitled, *Antiquities of the Jews*:

> *Now there was about this time Jesus, a wise man, for he was*
> *a doer of wonderful works, a teacher of such men as received*
> *the truth with pleasure. He drew over to him both many of*

the Jews and many Gentiles. When Pilate, at the suggestion of the principle men against us, had condemned him to the cross, those who loved him did not forsake him. And the tribe of Christians so named for him are not extinct to this day.[71]
—Book 18: Chapter 3

So it's quite clear that Jesus of Nazareth was an actual historical figure whose impact on his followers was significant. Nevertheless, how do we know him to be the actual Messiah that had been prophesied in the Bible?

As previously stated, there are about fifty different Messianic prophecies included in the Old Testament. They present us with more than 250 unique details that were fulfilled in the person of Jesus. In the Gospel of Luke, Jesus said the following:

He said to them, 'How foolish you are, and how slow to believe all that the prophets have spoken! Did not the Messiah have to suffer these things and then enter his glory?' And beginning with Moses and all the Prophets, he explained to them what was said in all the scriptures concerning himself.
—Luke 24:25-27

The disciples also witnessed many sights and miracles during their time with Jesus, but even they were slow to recognize his position as the prophesied Messiah. The following points of prophecy in the Old Testament concern Jesus' role as the "deliverer."

The Messiah would be born in Bethlehem.
—Micah 5:2

The Messiah would be born in the line of Jacob.
—Genesis 35:10-12

The Messiah would be born of the tribe of Judah.
—Genesis 49:10

The Messiah would be of the house of David.

—II Samuel 7:12-16

The Messiah would perform many miracles.

—Isaiah 35:5-6

The Messiah would speak in parables.

—Psalm 78:2

The Messiah would be rejected by his own people.

—Isaiah 8:14

The Messiah would come while the temple stands.

—Malachi 3:1

The Messiah would be betrayed for 30 pieces of silver.

—Zechariah 11:12

The Messiah would be resurrected from the dead.

—Psalm 16:10

These are only a few of the Old Testament prophecies that were fulfilled in the life, death, and resurrection of Jesus.

The Probabilities

In his thought provoking series known as the *Case for Christ,* an investigative journalist named Lee Strobel examined the evidence concerning Jesus. As a self-professed atheist, Strobel completed an extensive investigation of the evidence surrounding the case for Jesus as the prophesied Messiah. In this fascinating work, Strobel uncovered the following data:

A college professor of mathematics and astronomy named Dr. Peter Stoner wanted to determine what the odds were that any human being throughout human history could

*have fulfilled the messianic prophecies. In his study entitled,
"Science Speaks," Stoner presented his findings—estimating
that the odds of any single human being fulfilling 48 of these
ancient prophecies would be one chance in a trillion, trillion,
trillion, trillion, trillion, trillion, trillion, trillion, trillion,
trillion, trillion, trillion, trillion.*[72]

Those are astounding odds. While some of the prophecies alluded
to behavior on the part of Jesus, most of them described facts that were
beyond his control. For instance, how could the Old Testament prophet
Zechariah possibly know that Jesus would be betrayed some 500 years later
for thirty pieces of silver?

Strobel began his investigation as an atheist, but he completed it with
an appreciation for the evidence supporting the divinity of Jesus. He
concluded:

> *In light of the convincing facts that I had learned during
> my investigation, in the face of the overwhelming avalanche
> of evidence in the case for Christ, the great irony was this:
> it would require much more faith for me to maintain my
> atheism than to trust in Jesus of Nazareth.*[73]

The Lamb of God

If we can say with confidence that we understand who Jesus was, then
we can begin to reconcile his position within the context of Old Testament
thinking. We now understand that sin entered the world when Adam
and Eve deliberately disobeyed God in the Garden of Eden. Man then
lived under the Law of Moses for nearly 2,000 years, making ritual blood
sacrifices to atone for sins. *When Jesus came as the prophesied Messiah, his
blood sacrifice on the cross made temple sacrifice obsolete.* This means that all
of our sins have been effectively canceled by the blood offering of Jesus,
the aptly named Lamb of God. The Apostle Paul explained:

> *When you were dead in your sins and in the uncircumcision
> of the flesh, God made you alive with Christ. He forgave*

> us all of our sins, having canceled the charge of our legal
> indebtedness, which stood against us and condemned us; he
> has taken it away, nailing it to the cross.
>
> **—Colossians 2:13-14**

This single divine act redeemed believers for all of eternity. Therefore, the priests no longer needed to offer blood sacrifices on behalf of themselves and God's people. The writer of Hebrews concurred:

> Unlike the other high priests, he (Jesus) does not need to offer
> sacrifices day after day, first for his own sins, and then for
> the sins of the people. He sacrificed for their sins once for all
> when he offered himself.
>
> **—Hebrews 7:27**

There is no doubt that Jesus had the power to stop the process of his own crucifixion and punish those on earth who conspired to take his life. After all, if he had the power to command the winds and the waves, he certainly had the power to save himself. However, scripture affirms that he gave his life freely so that you and I might have the opportunity for redemption and eternal life. Ultimately, the sacrificial offering of Jesus (who had no sin) was orchestrated by God himself in order to reverse the damage done to mankind in the Garden of Eden. Again, the Apostle Paul said it best:

> For as in Adam all die, so in Christ all will be made alive.
>
> **—I Corinthians 15:22**

So what does all of this mean in the context of addiction? First and foremost, we now understand that addiction is driven by nothing more than behavior and choice. On some level, I think we are all aware that abusing substances is wrong, and can thus be categorized as sinful behavior. Remember: Substance abuse is not really any worse than any of our other sins, but it is unquestionably a sin. If we lived in the time of Moses, we would be required by God to offer a blood sacrifice to atone for our sins. But since Jesus did his work on the cross, our sins have effectively been canceled. All we need to do is accept his sacrifice on our behalf. In effect,

Jesus did the heavy lifting, but we get all the benefits of the effort. Dr. Gerald May finalizes the thought:

> *Jesus was the New Adam, the profound love gift of God entering the world to effect a reconciliation of humanity with God. ... He came for sinners who missed the mark of responding to God's love. To put it bluntly, God became incarnate to save the addicted, and that includes all of us.*[74]

CHAPTER FOURTEEN

Addiction, Repentance, and the Prodigal Son

It is not the healthy who need a doctor, but the sick. I have not come to call the righteous, but sinners to repentance.

—Jesus Christ
Luke 5:31

REPENTANCE IS AN easy concept to explain, but a difficult goal to achieve. When most people imagine repentance, they think of tearful admissions and heart wrenching apologies. But the idea of what it means to "repent" in the Bible is actually much simpler. While it does involve a confession of sorts, it primarily describes a process by which we transform our thoughts and actions entirely.

The New Testament (which literally means "New Covenant") was written primarily in Greek. So it is often helpful to look at the original Greek language used in the Gospels for clarity in the meanings of important passages. In Greek, the word used for "repent" means literally "a complete and total change of mind."[75] This definition indicates that in order to truly repent, we must deliberately "turn away" from our old way of life and strive to follow a new path.

The Parable of the Prodigal Son

Jesus often taught important principles of living within the subtle mechanisms of a parable. This term (derived from the Greek word *parabole*) means to "lay alongside." So a parable is a simple story that is told to illustrate a specific principle by laying alongside the real meaning. Jesus used such stories to explain his teachings in ways that the average follower could understand. In this case, Jesus used the Parable of the Prodigal Son to illustrate the critical principle of repentance.

In this instance, Jesus was teaching a large group of followers when he told the following story. In the parable, a prosperous man was the father of two sons. Although it was customary for a father's estate to be divided upon his death, the younger son in this story asked for his share of the inheritance during his father's lifetime. This was a bold request because the firstborn son in antiquity would have precedence in any division of a father's estate as a simple function of his birthright. This would have been a shameful request for any son to have made and would have brought disgrace upon the family.

Nevertheless, Jesus explained that the father granted this unusual request and divided his property between his two sons. The younger son then set off for a distant country where he squandered his wealth on "wild living." A severe famine then overtook that country, and the son was forced to hire himself out as a laborer just to survive. As a servant, he was humbled greatly and forced to feed pigs in the fields. This would have been a major disgrace to any Jew because the Bible forbade Jews from owning, eating, or even being in the presence of pigs. According to the story:

> *He longed to fill his stomach with the pods that the pigs were eating, but no one gave him anything.*
> **—Luke 15:16**

At some point, the prodigal son's circumstances became so desperate that he longed to return to his father's household—not with the elevated status of a son, but as a humble servant.

When he came to his senses, he said, 'How many of my father's hired servants have food to spare, and here I am starving to death! I will set out and go back to my father and say to him: Father, I have sinned against heaven and against you. I am no longer worthy to be called your son; make me like one of your hired servants.' So he got up and went to his father.

—Luke 15:17-20

The younger son left the foreign land and set out on the journey home. As he approached his home, his father saw him and was overjoyed.

But while he was still a long way off, his father saw him and was filled with compassion for him; he ran to his son, threw his arms around him and kissed him.

—Luke 15:20

The son confessed his sins, and the father received him with open arms. In fact, he celebrated his return:

But the father said to his servants, 'Quick! Bring the best robe and put it on him. Put a ring on his finger and sandals on his feet. Bring the fattened calf and kill it. Let's have a feast and celebrate. For this son of mine was dead and is alive again; he was lost and is found.' So they began to celebrate.

—Luke 15:22-24

At this point in the narrative, the elder son came in from the field. Upon witnessing the celebration, the older brother was jealous and complained to his father:

Look! All these years I've been slaving for you and never disobeyed your orders. Yet you never gave me even a young goat so I could celebrate with my friends. But when this son of yours who has squandered your property with prostitutes comes home, you kill the fattened calf for him!

—Luke 15:29-30

The elder son was upset because the father was celebrating the return of his irresponsible little brother. The father, however, saw things differently:

> *'My son,' the father said, 'you are always with me, and everything I have is yours. But we had to celebrate and be glad, because this brother of yours was dead and is alive again: he was lost and is found.'*
>
> **—Luke 15:31-32**

The Meaning of the Story

This parable is one of the most popular illustrations of unconditional love and redemption in the Bible. Let's take a closer look at this story to discover its greater meaning in the context of addiction and sin.

First of all, it is important to match the main characters in the story with their intended roles. The character of the father is an obvious reference to God the Father. The older brother in the story is intended to represent the Jewish elite at the time of Jesus. And finally, the younger son represents sinners in need of forgiveness.

Jesus intended for the younger son to be a character to which we could all relate. At some point, we have all dishonored God by wasting our time on "wild living." We have all been guilty of disgracing our Father by placing our desires and cravings above all else. As so-called "addicts," we have been especially bold in doing so. We've taken the gifts we've been given (such as our talents and strengths) and squandered them by choosing personal pleasure over personal responsibility. We've heaped shame upon ourselves and our families, thinking little of how our actions have grieved our Heavenly Father.

God is just like the father in this story because He loves each of us as children … His children. And God doesn't just love us—He is "in love" with us. As a result, He has granted us the freedom to choose our own paths. When we fail to choose wisely, He grieves for us like any father grieves for a wayward child. In this parable, the father looked beyond the insults of the younger son, allowing him to receive his inheritance and venture out into the world on his own. He granted the son's request by giving him a portion of the wealth from his estate; despite the fact that he had yet to deserve it. You see—God stands by us at all times, even when we choose to worship ourselves and substances instead of Him.

The son then traveled to a faraway place, creating a great deal of distance between himself and his father. In much the same way, when we act in opposition to God's will for our lives, we experience spiritual separation from God. When we behave in inappropriate and foolish ways, we naively consider ourselves to be beyond our Father's reach.

Furthermore, I cannot imagine a more classic example of "wild living" than a chemical fueled binge. When we are entangled in an endless cycle of substance abuse, we think little of the long term consequences. We often experience the *famines* of life in much the same way—and end up *hungry and lost* as we look for a way out. We often do shameful, humiliating things to support our habits and feed our substance starving souls.

The hopeful message of this parable begins when the son finally comes to his senses. In the King James translation of this passage, the text says, "he came to himself." In simple terms, Jesus was saying that the son recognized his sins and realized what he had become. He then reconsidered his position, deciding to *turn away* from his old life and turn toward home. The son understood that he could no longer continue his wild ways, and began the fateful journey home. He made the humbling personal choice to return to his father—which is the essence of repentance. Upon his return, the father's love, compassion, and grace facilitated complete restoration.

Come to Yourself

In a similar way, we need to "come to ourselves" and evaluate our own positions in life. We can continue our riotous living and suffer the consequences, or we can admit our mistakes and seek reconciliation with God the Father. Pastor Francis Chan explains:

> *Some people encounter Jesus and say, 'Sweet Jesus, do you want to join the party of my life with this sin, that addiction, this destructive relationship, and we'll all just coexist together?' But repentance means saying, 'Sweet Jesus, you are the best thing that has ever happened to me! I want to turn from all the sin and selfishness that rules me.*[76]

If we truly desire a renewed relationship with God the Father, we need to recognize our compromised states and learn to cast aside our stubborn appetites. After turning away from our addictive choices, we can begin the journey home to healing and wholeness.

As human beings, we often distance ourselves from the Lord and expect to have God do all the work to bring us back. This, however, is not how the process works. Consider for a moment a football analogy. Many people prefer to play a game that I call "Quarterback Christianity." This simply means that we as Christians wish to drop back to pass like the great Joe Namath, make a short throw to the Lord and have Him carry the ball all the way down the field for a touchdown. In other words, we are willing to participate somewhat in the restoration process, but we have no real interest in breaking a sweat along the way. We want to call the play, but we ask God to do all of the work to accomplish the goal.

True redemption and repentance involve a willingness on our part to get our hands a little dirty. We must decide to make a change and then put forth genuine effort toward carrying the ball into the end-zone of life. We can't ask the Lord to do all the hard work while we stand by and admire the process from the sidelines. We must "get in the game" and show the drive and determination to finish the race on our own.

The best news of all is that we never have to worry about traveling this road alone. The father in the parable, knowing that his son wanted to return home, was willing to meet him on the road. This same spiritual courtesy is offered to each of us. When we are "still a long way off," God the Father will meet us on the road with a loving, passionate embrace.

Fortunately, we will not have to finish the journey or make the accompanying transformation alone, because God will take each step with us and provide a scriptural road map as a guide. *Most importantly, we don't have to be fixed to come back to God, we only need to make a commitment to meet Him along the way.* Then the process of healing our minds, bodies, and souls can truly begin. Furthermore, we will not be punished or made to pay a penalty for our misdeeds upon our return. God will meet us on the road with open arms and demonstrate exuberant joy regardless of the reception we deserve.

Also, if any other "brothers" express reservations, the Father will come to our defense. The older son in this story represents the Jewish elite at the time, who no doubt felt that the Gentiles (non-Jews) did not deserve the Father's love. In a similar way, there are people in our own lives who will judge us and express jealousy when we turn from our depravity and shame.

Thankfully, God is not like us. His capacity for forgiveness and compassion knows no bounds! *He wants nothing more than for us to turn away from our sins and turn toward Him.* While we most certainly have at some point been lost, we may just as easily be found in the arms of a God who loves us unconditionally. The road home may be littered with perils and temptations, but arriving at our destination will be rewarding and worthwhile. Addiction Psychologist Dr. Gerald May said it best:

> *Therefore, the journey homeward does not lead toward new, more sophisticated addictions. If it is truly homeward, it leads toward liberation from addiction altogether.*[77]

The year was 1993. Kevin and I were in a small church in Mississippi listening to a sermon on the Prodigal Son. I was familiar with the story, but the definition of "prodigal" was never clear to me. In the context of the parable, I assumed the term meant "stupid or foolish."

Kevin had returned again from the abusive abyss following months of active drug use to try and get clean. He did so periodically, whenever he ran out of money or became so fatigued by the intensity of the lifestyle that he could no longer endure it. His physical condition had greatly deteriorated, and his thought processes and memory were compromised. He was weak and alarmingly malnourished. His eyes held the vacant look of a corpse. He had not bathed in weeks, and he had lost all of his possessions, returning with only the clothes on his back.

Whenever he stayed with me, there were two main rules: he could not "use" substances of any kind, and he needed to attend church services with me three times a week. This particular week was different because our church was holding its semi-annual revival, which meant that we attended church every night for five days in a row.

As we sat there listening to a rousing message on redemption and forgiveness, the minister explained the definition of the term "prodigal." The word was used in a biblical context to describe someone who "wasted his/her talents or gifts." This made more sense to me and seemed to strike a chord in the ever sobering mind of my brother. Kevin had always been a good athlete and later had discovered an enviable talent in creating and performing music. He played the guitar and a few other instruments quite well, and he also had a gift for writing songs.

As we drove home after the service, we talked for a while about the message. I sheepishly admitted that I hadn't really known the actual meaning of the word "prodigal." Kevin spoke about his love of music and voiced his wish that some parts of his life had been different. After a few minutes of intense silence, he said something that I'll never forget. "I can relate to the dude in that story. That guy, the prodigal son, that's me!"

CHAPTER FIFTEEN

The Apostle Paul and the Gift of Salvation

I am the way and the truth and the life. No one comes to the Father except through me.

—Jesus Christ
John 14:6

N OW THAT WE have established the importance of repentance as it relates to addiction, we need to consider the next steps in the spiritual process of salvation. Nearly everyone is familiar with the sentiments expressed in the popular passage that follows:

For God so loved the world that he gave his one and only Son, that whoever believes in him shall not perish but have eternal life.

—John 3:16

The very next verse is far less familiar, but no less important in our understanding of God's plan.

For God did not send his Son into the world to condemn the world, but to save the world through him.

—John 3:17

Jesus, who bore the sins of mankind on the cross, was offered by God as the final sacrifice. This ultimate gift of redemption is available to all who faithfully accept Jesus Christ as the Savior of their lives. Obviously, repentance is an essential step in our reconciliation with God. But if we don't actively pursue a relationship with Jesus, his sacrifice is meaningless for us. In order to complete the salvation process and guarantee our positions in God's eternal kingdom, we must trust in Jesus as the Lord of our lives.

Paul of Tarsus

The Apostle Paul is a perfect example of how the process of redemption works. First and foremost, he recognized his role as a sinner. He realized that the way he lived his life brought shame upon God the Father:

> *Here is a trustworthy saying that deserves full acceptance: Christ Jesus came into the world to save sinners—of whom I am the worst. But for that very reason I was shown mercy so that in me, the worst of sinners, Christ Jesus might display this immense patience as an example for those who would believe in him and receive eternal life.*
> **—I Timothy 1:15-16**

Paul stated that he was the best example ever of someone whose behavior displeased God, which is clear when we examine his checkered past.

Prior to his conversion, Paul was known by his Hebrew name—Saul of Tarsus. He was a Pharisee, aptly referred to as a "Hebrew of Hebrews," and a well-known member of the Jewish elite. But before he became a Christian, he spent most of his time speaking against the faith. In fact, he enthusiastically persecuted the early followers of Jesus on a grand scale. He even assisted in the stoning of Stephen (the first Christian martyr), who was a gifted speaker and a prominent follower of Christ. As someone who aggressively persecuted the followers of Jesus, his actions were instrumental in stunting the growth of the early Christian church.

One day, Saul (as he was known then) was traveling from Jerusalem to Damascus to arrest and prosecute followers of Jesus. All of a sudden, he had an encounter on the road with the post-resurrection Christ that changed his life forever. Luke tells the story:

> *As he neared Damascus on his journey, suddenly a light from heaven flashed around him. He fell to the ground and heard a voice say to him, 'Saul, Saul, why do you persecute me?' 'Who are you Lord?' Saul asked. 'I am Jesus, whom you are persecuting,' he replied. 'Now get up and go into the city, and you will be told what you must do.'*
>
> **—Acts 9:3-6**

The men traveling with him were very afraid because they also heard the voice but did not see anyone speaking. When Saul got up from the ground, he opened his eyes but could not see. He was then led blind into the city where he was met by a follower of Christ named Ananias.

> *Then Ananias went to the house and entered it. Placing his hands on Saul, he said, 'Brother Saul, the Lord—Jesus, who appeared to you on the road as you were coming here—has sent me so that you may see again and be filled with the Holy Spirit.' Immediately, something like scales fell from Saul's eyes, and he could see again. He got up and was baptized, and after taking some food, he regained his strength.*
>
> **—Acts 9:17-19**

Saul then took his Roman name Paul and began boldly preaching in the synagogues and gathering places proclaiming Jesus as the prophesied Messiah.

Paul's life is a excellent example of the patience and compassion of God. Before he came to know Jesus as Christ, he was one of the greatest enemies of the early Christian movement. Following the call of Jesus, he repented of his sins and dedicated his life in service to God by spreading the message of salvation. Not only was Paul one of the greatest missionaries in history, but he would go on to become one of the most prolific writers in the Bible. His letters account for nearly two-thirds of the content in the New Testament and have inspired countless people to find peace through Christ.

The Simplicity of Salvation

In the Book of Romans, Paul outlined the basic process of achieving salvation:

> *If you declare with your mouth, 'Jesus is Lord,' and believe*
> *in your heart that God raised him from the dead, you will*
> *be saved.*
>
> **—Rom 10:9**

Remarkably, salvation is that simple. We must decide to put Jesus first in our lives and forsake our prior entanglements in sin. We must also believe that Jesus was born of the virgin Mary, having been conceived by the Holy Spirit. We must accept as fact that he lived on the earth in human form and that he died a bodily death by crucifixion. We must confess that he was resurrected on the third day and that he ascended into heaven. If this affirmation of faith is declared with sincerity, salvation and eternal life are guaranteed. This awesome gift is available to all those who choose to believe!

Born Again—Say Again?

Now let's take a closer look at the concept of being *born again*. It can be confusing in terms of theology, but it is crucially important in developing a strategy for controlling ongoing behaviors like addiction.

In the days prior to his crucifixion, Jesus taught and preached around the temple in Jerusalem. He spent hours instructing his followers in the faith and sparring with the Jewish authorities on subjects related to his ministry. A man named Nicodemus was a Pharisee and a respected member of the Jewish ruling council. He and others acknowledged Jesus as a teacher who had come from God, because they reasoned that no one could perform the kinds of miraculous signs and wonders unless God was with them.

Away from the temple complex, Nicodemus met secretly with Jesus to have questions regarding his teachings answered. In the course of the conversation, Jesus revealed the one and only way to experience the kingdom of God:

> *Jesus declared, 'Very truly I tell you, no one can see the kingdom of God unless they are born again.' 'How can someone be born when they are old?' Nicodemus asked. 'Surely they cannot enter a second time into their mother's womb to be born!' Jesus answered, 'Very truly I tell you, no one can enter the kingdom of God unless they are born of water and the Spirit. Flesh gives birth to flesh, but the Spirit gives birth to spirit.'*
>
> **—John 3:3-6**

This scripture is an example of Jesus' inclination toward symbolism in his ministry. When he spoke these words to Nicodemus, he fully intended to shock him. The concept of being *born again* was unlike anything that had been taught before in the synagogues or Jewish history. This was fresh theology based on becoming a new (or changed) person committed to supporting the kingdom of God.

In the language of the time, the Greek translation of the term *born again* likely meant to be "born from above."[78] In essence, Jesus was telling Nicodemus that you have to let your old self die and experience a spiritual rebirth of sorts to become bound to the Lord.

This idea may have come from a passage written by the Old Testament prophet Ezekiel. In it God declares:

> *I will give them (God's people) an undivided heart and put a new spirit in them; I will remove from them their heart of stone and give them a heart of flesh. Then they will follow my decrees and be careful to keep my laws.*
>
> **—Ezekiel 11:19-20**

In this passage, God was telling the nation of Israel that in spite of their disloyalty, He would provide them with a new heart and an improved spirit which would be more willing to obey. In the same way, God offers to take away your stubborn, inflexible addictive desires by removing your *heart of stone.* Our hearts will then be softened into flesh and will become more flexible and open to correction. We will then be more amenable to the changes God desires in our way of life.

When we come to accept Jesus as our personal sacrifice for sin, we are given a brand new nature. In essence, we are *born again* with this new nature as we cast aside the old nature (which we received at birth), the one sullied by sin in the Garden of Eden. Our old nature must die at the time of our Christian conversion, and we must commit to the internal changes required by God. Our salvation has then been justified by Christ Jesus on the cross. The Apostle Paul affirmed this:

> *For we know that our old self was crucified with him so that the body ruled by sin might be done away with, that we should no longer be slaves to sin—because anyone who has died has been set free from sin.*
>
> **—Romans 6:6-7**

This is where the process of repentance and salvation relate directly to our struggles with addiction. In order to win this battle, we must accept the fact that our old fleshly desires can be removed. It then becomes possible to clothe ourselves in the *garment of salvation* whenever we forge a new relationship with Jesus. We are reborn from above ... in sync with God and His plan. With a heart willing to make changes, we will then be empowered to cast aside our addictions and sinful preoccupations with drugs and alcohol.

Let Go of the Past

As Christians, we are no longer held responsible for the original sin of mankind. With the help of Jesus, we are given a new spirit to help us deal with our shortcomings. *However, change is not just suggested—it is required by God.* These changes in us are mandated by the Lord; they are not a matter of preference on our part. Again, Paul explains:

> *You were taught with regard to your former way of life, to put off your old self, which is being corrupted by its deceitful desires; to be made new in the attitude of your minds; and to put on the new self, created to be like God in true righteousness and holiness.*
>
> **—Ephesians 4:22-24**

If God requires us to change, don't you think He'll make arrangements to help us along the way? He doesn't expect us to say a simple prayer and change our behavior on our own. It is God's provision of the Holy Spirit that enables us to keep our old self in the grave. The Apostle Paul said:

> *Therefore, if anyone is in Christ, the new creation has come: the old has gone, the new is here!*
>
> **—II Corinthians 5:17**

Jesus said the following in the Gospel of Luke:

> *No one who puts a hand to the plow and looks back is fit for service in the kingdom of God.*
>
> **—Luke 9:62**

With those words, the Messiah was telling us that looking backwards serves no purpose. In other words, we are not to obsess about the reckless decisions we made in the past. We cannot dwell on those mistakes, since it could affect how well we serve the kingdom of God in the future.

Without question, this is more easily said than done. Many of us have great difficulty letting go of the past. We often cannot forgive ourselves for selfish behaviors, and we carry the weight of this burden forward each and every day. This is why the concept of being *born again* has so much value. You need to put the reality of your old behaviors in the rear view mirror of life, and you need to let go of the accompanying guilt. You cannot go back in time and repair all that has been broken, but you can commit to making a change in your body and spirit as you move forward. Drop the burdens of your past by the roadside as you continue your journey, racing with enthusiasm and hope toward the finish-line of freedom!

God has forgiven you—now you need to forgive yourself! You have to release your firm grip on the baggage of your past. Having done so, the path that lies ahead becomes free of a major obstacle preventing personal growth and success. The Reverend Billy Graham concludes:

> *While the works of the flesh would like very much to manifest themselves—and sometimes do—they no longer reign, they are no longer in control. It is no longer a practice; it is no longer a habit; we are transformed by his grace and live the new life in Christ.*[79]

If you have not done so, I urge you now to seize this opportunity to achieve salvation through Jesus. You have nothing to lose except your former destructive lifestyle. *If you wish to continue worshiping drugs and alcohol as your gods, then I would suggest you not embrace God's plan. When you are truly born again, you'll find that you become more interested in pleasing God than pleasing yourself.*

The most important Tuesday of Kevin's life began like any other day. The year was 2000 and he was staying with my family again, fresh from another disappointing attempt at rehab. He was working with me at our automotive business in Northeast Mississippi. He was always a hard worker and fit in well with the rest of our crew. Early that afternoon, I had gone to the warehouse to check on something. As I headed back toward the sales area, I noticed that Kevin was sitting behind the desk in my office with his head buried in his hands.

The expression on his face was similar to the one he wore in Washington DC as the elevator doors closed. There was a look of sadness and bewilderment in his eyes that told me that something was seriously wrong. Choking back tears, he explained that one of his best friends from the streets had just been killed in a drive-by shooting in the city of Chicago. His friend had simply been in the wrong place at the wrong time, paying for this mistake with his life. I stood in stunned silence, not knowing what to say.

After a moment or two, I asked him what he wanted to do next. His response surprised me. "I can't live like this anymore. That could have easily have been me. I'm ready to make a change, and I'm ready to make it now!" Although I had waited for many years to hear those words, my reaction was one of stunned silence. When I finally responded, I told him that we could take care of everything in a few days at church. He responded with a sense of urgency, "No, you don't understand. I need to do it now!"

Within the hour, we gathered together in the living room of our home. Kevin explained his wishes to us, and we knelt down in prayer as a family. He spoke in his own words, admitting his faults and asking Jesus to forgive him. He asked to be transformed that day into something different—someone totally new. At that time and in that place, my brother Kevin gave his life to the Lord. We hugged each other with tears in our eyes and celebrated his very first moments as a Christian. It was one of the most authentic and powerful events that I have ever witnessed.

PART III

Addiction and the Holy Spirit

A born-again Christian should no more think of going back to the old life than an adult to his childhood, a married man to his bachelorhood, or a discharged prisoner to his prison cell.

—Dr. John Stott
Acclaimed Author and Theologian

CHAPTER SIXTEEN

What the Heck is the Holy Spirit?

Now the Lord is the Spirit, and where the Spirit of the Lord is, there is freedom.

—The Apostle Paul
II Corinthians 3:17

B Y NOW, MOST people are familiar with the concept of the Holy Trinity. The first two members of the Trinity are easily identifiable. God (The Father) created the universe and controls everything within it. Jesus (The Son) lived in the flesh on the earth as a human being who became the sacrificial offering for sin.

However, the third member of the Trinity has always seemed harder to comprehend. It is the ever-present entity known as the Holy Spirit. The Spirit's coming was prophesied in the Old Testament and also by Jesus prior to his death on the cross. If we are to fully appreciate the divine nature of God, we must acquire an understanding of what the Holy Spirit is and what role it plays in our daily walk with the Lord.

As we work our way through the study of the Bible, we should begin to understand the emphasis placed on each member of the Holy Trinity in the larger context of scripture. For the most part, the works of God the Father are emphasized in the stories and language of the Old Testament. We learned how the universe was created; and we learned that God has loved and nurtured us throughout the history of mankind.

The works of Jesus are especially emphasized in the Gospels at the beginning of the New Testament. We learned how Jesus was born; who he was; and how he gave his life for the forgiveness of sins. Although the Gospels tell his story in somewhat different ways, their overall message is consistent. Jesus is God's divine "deliverer," who was offered to save us all from our sinful selves.

Beginning with the Book of Acts, the remainder of the New Testament has been presented for the primary purpose of describing the workings of the Holy Spirit. The reality of the Spirit of God is proclaimed with emphasis in these remaining books. We will now discover the identity of this entity; where it came from; and what its primary purpose is in the lives of Christians.

If God is the Father and Jesus is the Son, then the Holy Spirit is the authentic "Spirit of God." According to scripture, it is a distinct entity that stands on it's own. Although it is endowed with the qualities of both the Father and the Son, it is also an independent spiritual force unlike the others.

The Holy Trinity has been described in comparison with the natural states of water. Water can exist in three separate forms: as a liquid in its natural form (God), as a solid in its more material form (Jesus), and as a gas like water vapor in its most effervescent form (the Holy Spirit). All three forms of water are identical in terms of composition, but very different in terms of their appearance and purpose. In much the same way, *the three members of the Holy Trinity are one in the same but very different in the ways in which they manifest in our lives.*

The Holy Spirit and Pentecost

Jesus introduced his disciples to the concept of the Holy Spirit prior to his crucifixion. In scripture, Jesus referred to another "Comforter" or "Advocate" that was to come. In the original Greek, "advocate" meant 'another that is just like the first.' This purposeful use of language by Jesus told his disciples that this entity would be very much like him. Jesus proclaimed the following:

And I will ask the Father, and He will give you another advocate to help you and be with you forever—the Spirit of truth. The world cannot accept him, because it neither sees him or knows him. But you know him, for he lives with you and will be in you.

—John 14:16-17

Those words tell us that the Holy Spirit would not be visible but would take up residence within the hearts of believers. Jesus continued:

But very truly I tell you, it is for your good that I am going away. Unless I go away, the Advocate will not come to you; but if I go, I will send him to you. When he comes, he will prove the world to be in the wrong about sin and righteousness and judgment.

—John 16:7-8

In that passage, Jesus was telling us that one of the most important functions of this Spirit would lie in its ability to convict us of sin in our lives. Finally, Jesus stated:

But when he, the Spirit of truth comes, he will guide you in all the truth. He will not speak on his own; he will only speak what he hears, and he will tell you what is yet to come. He will glorify me because it is from me that he will receive what he will make known to you.

—John 16:13-14

Jesus concluded this prophetic announcement by telling us that the Spirit would be given to communicate divine truths to believers on the most fundamental levels. This Spirit would come upon us like the cleansing waters of baptism and be a guaranteed gift from God for those who choose to be *born again*. In fact, Jesus spoke the following words after the resurrection to his disciples just before he ascended to heaven:

Do not leave Jerusalem, but wait for the gift my Father promised, which you have heard me speak about. For John

> *baptized with water, but in a few days you will be baptized*
> *with the Holy Spirit. … But you will receive power when*
> *the Holy Spirit comes on you; and you will be my witnesses*
> *in Jerusalem, and in all Judea and Samaria, and to the ends*
> *of the earth.*
>
> **—Acts 1:4-5; 7-8**

The apostles (from the Greek word meaning "messengers") obeyed Jesus and stayed in Jerusalem after the ascension. They were still fearful of the Jewish and Roman authorities, so they met secretly out of the public eye. They chose a devout man named Matthias to replace the former disciple, Judas Iscariot, who died in the midst of the events surrounding the crucifixion. They gathered with 120 other followers in an upper room fifty days or so after the resurrection to pray and await direction from the Lord.

> *Suddenly a sound like the blowing of a violent wind came*
> *from heaven and filled the whole house where they were*
> *sitting. They saw what seemed to be tongues of fire that*
> *separated and came to rest on each of them. All of them were*
> *filled with the Holy Spirit and began to speak in other tongues*
> *as the Spirit enabled them.*
>
> **—Acts 2:2-4**

The Bible says that a large group of "God-fearing Jews" from every nation heard the sounds and gathered at the scene. When they heard the apostles declaring the wonders of God in many different languages, they were amazed. They were astonished because the disciples were simple men who were not educated in foreign languages. The Apostle Peter then gave a rousing sermon to the crowd, preaching the doctrine of salvation in Christ Jesus. Peter proclaimed:

> *Repent and be baptized, every one of you, in the name of Jesus*
> *Christ for the forgiveness of your sins. And you will receive the*
> *gift of the Holy Spirit. The promise is for you and your children*
> *who are far off—for all whom the Lord our God will call.*
>
> **—Acts 2:38-39**

Scripture proclaims that about three thousand people accepted salvation on that day and received the baptism of the Holy Spirit.

The Holy Spirit rained down upon the apostles and thousands of converts that day in an event that would come to be known as "Pentecost" (which is Greek meaning "fiftieth"). Just as Jesus had foretold, the actual Spirit of God descended from heaven on these early Christians. The apostles received the gifts of healing, spoke in tongues, and went forth boldly proclaiming the power and authority of God.

The Essence of the Holy Spirit

The very same Spirit that fell upon them will fall on you when you accept through faith the sacrificial work of Jesus on the cross. The Holy Spirit is also known as the "divine Paraclete," which means "one who walks by our side as our counselor, helper, defender, and guide."[80] The Bible states the following:

The Holy Spirit is God, himself.

—Acts 5:3-4

The Holy Spirit is ever-present.

—Psalm 139:7

The Holy Spirit is all-powerful.

—Luke 1:35

The Holy Spirit is all-knowing.

—I Corinthians 2:10-11

When we experience the salvation of Christ, God grants us the gift of this Holy Spirit as a bonus. According to scripture, the Spirit seals our relationship with God. In antiquity, a seal represented a covenant relationship, one which involves ownership. Reverend Billy Graham explained:

> *We can see that God places a seal on us when we receive*
> *Christ. And that seal is a person—the Holy Spirit. By the*
> *Spirit's presence God gives us security and establishes his*
> *ownership over us. Further, the Spirit is God's pledge. He not*
> *only seals the arrangement, but he represents God's voluntary*
> *obligation to see us through.*[81]

God wants all of us to follow Him and remain faithful to His will. Because He created us, He knows that we cannot win the fight against sin (and addiction) on our own. In His divine mercy and grace, God grants believers the marvelous gift of the Holy Spirit to reside within us and guide us along the way.

The single most important function of the Holy Spirit in the context of addiction is that it helps to convict us of our sins. When we are *born again* and are baptized with the presence of the Holy Spirit, we become more aware of the defects in our natural character. Through the direction of the Spirit, our sins and negative behaviors come to light. In this way, they are illuminated as being in opposition to our new-found commitment to conduct our lives in ways that honor God. Consequently, sins (and by extension substance abuse) become a painful thorn in our side—one that we no longer choose to endure. By the power of the Holy Spirit, we recognize the need to alter our behaviors and lifestyles accordingly. Billy Graham says it best:

> *A life touched by the Holy Spirit will tolerate sin no longer.*[82]

This is especially true of sins (like addiction) that we have previously been unable to overcome by our own strength. For many of us, adultery and covetousness don't have the appeal of a beer or bag of heroin. If you've not yet been able to bring your behavior under control, I urge you not to refuse spiritual help in the form of the Holy Spirit. Again, Billy Graham comments:

> *It is interesting that we often say someone is 'under the*
> *influence' of alcohol. Now that is somewhat the meaning of*
> *being filled with the Spirit. We are 'under the influence' of*

the Spirit. Instead of doing things with our own strength or
ability, He empowers us. Instead of doing only what we want
to do, we are now guided by Him.[83]

The Holy Spirit has the power to illuminate our minds. Since it lives inside us, the Spirit can see our dangerous darkness from within. The Spirit will identify these internal imperfections and help us to avoid situations that may test our resolve. Accepting the Holy Spirit is like unleashing an internal vacuum cleaner that seeks out all the dirt in us and removes it.

CHAPTER SEVENTEEN

"Obey" Shouldn't Be A Four Letter Word

Like a city whose walls are broken through is a person who lacks self-control.

—King Solomon
Proverbs 25:28

THE IDEA OF turning control of our lives over to an entity like the Holy Spirit can be a frightening proposition, indeed. Having previously discussed the AA doctrine of the "higher power," we are somewhat familiar with the concept ... but likely terrified at the prospect. Nevertheless, we should be willing to take a moment and realize the eternal value of handing the reigns of life over to the Spirit of the Living God.

If you're like me, you've had very little success in controlling your addictions on your own. You have fought this battle for years, spending so much time in secular rehabilitation and counseling that the thought of another attempt seems intolerable. I ask you now to consider accepting the salvation of Jesus so that you may have immediate access to the most underrated spiritual power in the universe.

The Holy Spirit can cleanse you of immoral thoughts and behaviors in an immediate and supernatural way. It can help you seize control of your actions in such a miraculous way that the changes are not even difficult to make. *The Holy Spirit, as one of its functions, was given the very key to unlock the stubborn door of addiction! So why not place your trust in the gift that God has granted believers for that specific purpose?*

When you are saved, the Holy Spirit will guide you somewhat like a harbor pilot guides large ships into ports of call. I have a friend in South Carolina who does this for a living. When a large vessel arrives at the mouth of the harbor, he rides a tugboat out and takes over the helm of the ship. He knows where the channels are treacherous and steers the ship away from danger. Since he knows the depths of the water, he prevents ships from running aground in the imperceptible shallows.

In much the same way, the Holy Spirit will take charge of your life and help steer you away from danger and irresponsible choices. The difference is that the Holy Spirit is not a requirement, but a gift! If you decide to trust in Jesus, you get the added services and expertise of the Holy Spirit at no additional charge. It can help you avoid perilous obstacles in your path and keep you from running aground. If you willingly accept the Spirit's guidance, you'll find your actions falling more in line with the divine will of God.

The Fruit of the Spirit

The Apostle Paul gave us further details on the supernatural benefits of being indwelt with the Holy Spirit. The following passage introduces the popular concept of the "fruit of the Spirit."

> *The acts of the flesh are obvious: sexual immorality; impurity and debauchery; idolatry and witchcraft; hatred, discord, jealousy, fits of rage, selfish ambition, dissensions, factions, and envy; drunkenness, orgies and the like. ... But the fruit of the Spirit is love, joy, peace, forbearance (patience), kindness, goodness, faithfulness, gentleness and self-control.*
> **—Galatians 5:19-23**

This scripture is important because it begins by revealing the emotions that ruled us as we were piloted by our old self ... governed by the flesh. It's interesting to note that the Greek word translated as "witchcraft" in this passage is *pharmakeia,* which is the root word of the modern term *pharmacy.*

The second half of the scripture introduces us to the feelings that we are likely to experience when our wills have become subservient to the will of the Holy Spirit. When our lives are piloted by the Spirit of God, we are more likely to exhibit these divine qualities in abundance. The first eight "fruits" of the presence of the Spirit are similar in nature. When the Holy Spirit takes charge of your life, you'll undoubtedly be a kinder, more loving, compassionate person.

The final "fruit of the Spirit" on the list is self-control. One cannot overstate the importance of self-control in avoiding a vicious cycle of substance abuse. The word in the original Greek translation for "self-control" means to "be strong, to master, to control one's thoughts and actions."[84] In terms of addiction, the presence of the Holy Spirit has been granted to believers so that we can supercharge our ability to muster greater confidence and self-control. Your ability to say "no" to your substance of choice will be turbocharged, meaning that you'll get better results from the same amount of effort.

As someone who was unable to control substances on your own, the active presence of the Holy Spirit will empower you to overcome their dominance in your life. The all-powerful Spirit of God will fight beside you as you wage a personal war against addiction. Even though we all possess the power of free will, you will be less likely to make destructive choices without feeling remorse or guilt. The voice inside you will be the actual voice of God.

In her book entitled, *Is That You God?*, Priscilla Shirer likens this voice to something you may have seen before:

> *All Christ's followers are equipped with a powerful tool that attunes our spiritual ears to the Lord's voice. The Holy Spirit is like an IFB— the tiny device news anchors wear in their ears so that their producers can guide their interviews and give them tips on how better to play to the camera.*[85]

This is a wonderful illustration of how the Holy Spirit communicates God's will. Instead of a producer, however, we have direct access to the thoughts and guidance of the genuine Spirit of God. The Spirit cannot be seen, but will offer advice on how to make better choices and live in concert with the purposes of God.

Even though we may still choose to sin, the Holy Spirit will continue guiding us and will speak words of encouragement in anticipation of the opportunity to win the next battle. When we choose poorly, we are most likely suppressing or ignoring the Spirit's commands, altogether. Life often moves at such a frantic pace that we feel as if we are losing control, like a runaway freight train barreling down the tracks. We sometimes move so fast that we don't take the time to stop and listen to the instructions of the Holy Spirit.

Since we are all flawed beings at heart, you may be forced to consider making choices that are outside of your comfort zone. However, *when you do make decisions in obedience to the voice of God, you will experience a great deal of peace.* For instance, if you are faced with a persistent temptation in the form of drugs or alcohol, the Spirit will guide you to abstain from its use. This may be contrary to what you want to hear, but it is certainly what you need to hear. Pastor Francis Chan, in his book entitled, *Forgotten God,* makes this clear:

> *The truth is that the Spirit of the living God is guaranteed to ask you to go somewhere or do something that you wouldn't normally want or choose to do. The Spirit will lead you to the way of the cross, as He led Jesus to the cross, and that is definitely not a safe or pretty or comfortable place to be. The Holy Spirit of God will mold you into the person you were made to be.*[86]

The Holy Spirit and Addiction

The Holy Spirit will also play a substantial role in fighting temptations and relapse. Here's how this works. When we are in the midst of a savage cyclone of substances, we often cannot remember making the decision to ingest our drug of choice. We recall the discomfort of withdrawal, but we have no recollection of making the conscious decision to actually use the substance. Previously, when thoughts of "using" entered our mind, we allowed the action of "using" to immediately follow. In other words, there

was very little separation between the thought and the action. Remember—
Even though the thought of using a substance may spark the mechanism of a craving, it does not have the power to necessitate an active response.

The action phase of substance abuse involves taking the steps necessary to acquire the substances, prepare them for use, and ingest them. This action phase does not always follow the thought instantaneously, which offers us the opportunity to change our minds and resist the urge to use. Having counseled individuals for years, I've had success in attempting to get substance abusers to examine their behavior in terms of this paradigm.

But first we must recognize that our choice to use chemicals involves both a thought and an action phase. Disease theorists would have you believe that these two phases are one in the same. In simple terms, the disease theory of addiction does not recognize your ability to separate the thoughts of using chemicals from the actual process of using them. Of course, when it comes to the realities of life, they are undoubtedly mistaken. *You may be unable (at this point) to control your thoughts regarding substances, but you most certainly can control the choice to initiate the action of using. No one else is to blame; and nothing else has the power to help control these actions like the genuine Spirit of God.*

When we accept this fact, we can attempt to try and separate these two phases from one another. For instance, imagine you are an "alcoholic" who has been in recovery for quite some time. In a moment of vulnerability, you experience an intense desire for a drink. Although you've been sober for months, you are obsessively thinking that you need alcohol right now. At this point, you find yourself at a crossroads. You must consciously choose whether or not to indulge your craving. That choice, whatever it is, becomes the action phase.

The best way to stifle the pangs of temptation is to separate the thought as far as possible from the action. The space "in between" is taken up by your capacity for choice and free will. This *wedge of choice* is the only thing standing between your desire for substances and your intention to abuse them. Most of us have found that our personal wedge is not strong enough to block the movement from the thought to the action phase. Either we consciously consider the choice, or we blindly proceed to the action phase in our search for an altered state of consciousness. In my view, this is precisely the point at which the power and presence of the Holy Spirit needs to be interjected.

Have you ever been going about the business of a normal day when you were assaulted by the most vile, detestable thought imaginable? You never intended for this thought to enter your mind, but you are forced to confront it, nonetheless. This is how cravings for drugs and alcohol often manifest in our minds. While some people constantly fantasize about intoxicating substances, most people try not to entertain those thoughts. Immoral thoughts (whether sexual or chemical in nature) cannot be totally expelled from our consciousness. *We cannot always control these thoughts, but we can control our reactions to them.* This is where the Holy Spirit enters the fray.

We need to attempt to fill the gap between the thought phase of our addiction and the action phase with insight from the Spirit of God. *When thoughts or cravings present themselves, we should take a moment to listen to the encouragement and guidance of the Holy Spirit. The Spirit that dwells within us will never instruct you to do anything that is contrary to the will of God.*

Priscilla Shirer wrote that our sinful nature acts like "radio static" and hinders our ability to hear the Spirit clearly.[87] I tend to agree. When we wish to return to a noisy cycle of chemical abuse, we cannot always hear the divine voice that is urging responsibility and abstinence. To be honest, we much prefer the simplicity of giving-in to our personal desires rather than making an effort to embrace the complexity of sobriety. This inclination toward sin generates a chaotic cluster of sound that makes it difficult to discern the voice of the Holy Spirit.

Do you know that humans have the remarkable ability to isolate individual sounds within blusterous clouds of "static?" Ironically, this auditory ability is known in scientific circles as the "cocktail party effect." It describes the innate ability of humans to focus their listening attention on a single voice among a bevy of background noise. This specialized listening ability has been recognized for years, although its not entirely understood from a scientific perspective.

Nevertheless, God has granted us this ability and we can make practical use of it in terms of addiction. If you concentrate fully, you can isolate the voice of the Spirit from the "cocktail party" of clutter around you. In doing so, you will hear the Lord's voice with clarity, in spite of the auditory "static" of others. However, it takes practice to block out this chaotic symphony and listen carefully to the singular voice of the Spirit.

Remember back to the story of the Hebrews exit from Egypt found in the second book of the Old Testament. We learned that Moses and the people had been driven to the edge of the Red Sea by the Egyptian army of Pharoah. They had no obvious means of escape; only divine intervention could save them. Just before God miraculously parted the waters, Moses told the people the following:

> *The Lord will fight for you; you need only to be still.*
> **—Exodus 14:13-14**

These words, spoken thousands of years ago, still ring with truth today. If you'll take the time to consider your choices and listen to the guidance of the Holy Spirit, God will fight the battle of addiction on your behalf. The Spirit of God will join you in the battle against cravings, helping you to be victorious in the war on substances as a whole. The Reverend Billy Graham made a similar point:

> *But never forget there will always be a struggle, both without and within. The devil is an implacable enemy. He never gives up. But I have the Holy Spirit within me. If I cooperate with Him and turn to Him for help, He will give me the power to resist temptation.*[88]

CHAPTER EIGHTEEN

The Devil and My Cutlass Supreme

Be alert and of sober mind. Your enemy the devil prowls
around like a roaring lion looking for someone to devour.

—The Apostle Peter
I Peter 5:8

ACCORDING TO RECENT public surveys, more than 90% of Americans believe in God. But according to those very same polls, only 57% of Americans believe in the devil.[89] This is a curious discrepancy, considering the sinister nature of the world around us. Why is this so, and what can be done to address this disparity?

As humans, it seems to be in our nature to dwell on the good rather than the bad. This can be problematic because life doesn't always end in "happily ever after." In reality, disharmony in life is the rule rather than the exception—and chaos is most often the result.

The biblical name for the architect of this chaos and the prince of this fallen world is Satan. The English transliteration of the Hebrew word "Satan" means "adversary," while the Greek word is most often translated as "hostile opponent."[90]

How do you picture the devil? Perhaps you envision some harmless version of a crimson comic book character holding a pitchfork. This popular image, which has been reinforced on television and in the movies, helps to set our minds at ease and creates the illusion that the devil is a matter of folly and not fact. In the minds of many, he dwells alongside fairies, leprechauns, and teenage wizards with magic wands. And that's right where the devil wants to be ... behind the wreckage and firmly out of view. Satan doesn't want us to actually believe in him—but he does want us to follow him.

In his book entitled, *The Screwtape Letters,* the great British writer, C.S. Lewis, tackled the concept of demons and the devil from a slightly different perspective. Lewis wrote letters in the name of a demon called Screwtape to another demonic entity regarding the spiritual battles waged for the souls of men. The demons made reference to humans as "patients," and they focused all their efforts on guiding them toward fellowship with their "Father Down Below." Lewis wrote the following words from one demon to another:

> *The fact that 'devils' are predominantly comic figures in the modern imagination will help you. If any faint suggestion of your existence begins to arise in his (the patient's) mind, suggest to him a picture of something in red tights, and persuade him that since he cannot believe in that (it is an old textbook method of confusing them) he therefore cannot believe in you.*[91]

In this way, the devil's most effective tactic for sowing the seeds of discord on earth is to convince us that he doesn't even exist. But do not be deceived. The devil does exist and one of his primary functions is to entice us to sin against God. *You're foolish not to believe in the devil, because he certainly believes in you.*

The Spirit Realm is Real

I'm not the kind of person who sees the devil behind every door. If you suffer a case of the sniffles or get a flat tire, Satan is not likely to blame. However, some people try to spiritualize everything, and in the process blame the devil for all the difficulties in their lives. Although this idea has no basis in scripture, this behavior can make Christians sound paranoid and a little crazy. Nevertheless, the Bible is quite clear in stating that angels, demons, and the devil definitely exist.

The attitude of most people on this subject brings to mind an account from the Bible's Old Testament in the book of Second Kings. That book, which was written sometime after the reign of King David but before the Babylonian exile, tells the story of a prophet named Elisha.

In the story, the King of Aram was fighting a war against King Joram and the nation of Israel. The prophet Elisha was counseling King Joram during the battles and delivering direct instructions from God. As a result, things were not going well for the army of Aram. Their ruthless king reasoned that by capturing and killing Elisha the tide would turn and he would surely win the war. So he sent a large force of chariots and soldiers overnight to the city of Dothan where Elisha was headquartered.

The next morning, Elisha's servant awoke in Dothan and realized that the enemy had arrived during the night and surrounded the city. Not surprisingly, he panicked and rushed to tell Elisha of their terrible predicament. Elisha responded dispassionately:

> *'Don't be afraid,' the prophet answered. 'Those who are with us are more than those who are with them.' And Elisha prayed, 'Open his eyes, Lord, so that he may see.' Then the Lord opened the servant's eyes, and he looked and saw the hills full of horses and chariots of fire all around Elisha.*
> **—II Kings 6:16-17**

In this story, the Lord had foreseen Elisha's circumstances and sent an army of angels to his aide. The invading soldiers were then blinded by God and led away from the city, thereby ending their occupation in Israeli territory.

This account is interesting because it represents the attitude that most people have with regard to the reality of the spirit world. The servant's reaction is natural and understandable in any context. When God "opened the servant's eyes," he could see the angelic provisions that had been made for their protection.

Along those lines, millions of people profess a belief in the existence of guardian angels. There have been numerous stories told over the years that involved the supernatural intervention of these angelic beings on behalf of people from all parts of the world. Not surprisingly, the concept of guardian angels does have a basis in scripture. The following words were likely written by a priest or temple worker in the Book of Psalms:

> *If you say, 'The Lord is my refuge,' and you make the Most High your dwelling, no harm will overtake you, no disaster will come near your tent. For he will command his angels concerning you to guard you in all your ways; they will lift you up in their hands, so that you will not strike your foot against a stone.*
> **—Psalm 91:9-12**

Today, many stories involving angelic intercession are told by people who are not especially spiritual. In most cases, however, these divine encounters have been instrumental in drawing people closer to the Lord. If you are one of the many who believe strongly in the existence of angels, then you need to understand that there is another side to the story. If you believe in angels, then you're foolish not to believe in demons and the devil.

Who and What is Satan?

The story of the devil and why he exists tells us everything we need to know about the problems of the world today. The Bible states that Satan was created by God as a specific type of angel. In the following passage, God explains this fact in the words of the prophet Ezekiel:

> *You were the model of perfection, full of wisdom and perfect in beauty. ... You were anointed as a guardian cherub, for so I ordained you. You were on the holy mount of God.*
> **—Ezekiel 28:12,14**

It is clear from this passage that things started out well in heaven between God and Satan. As an angelic creation, the devil was beautiful in appearance and "full of wisdom."

At some point, however, Lucifer (which means "son of the morning") decided that instead of serving God ... he wanted to be like God.

> *You (Lucifer) said in your heart, 'I will ascend to the heavens; I will raise my throne above the stars of God; I will sit enthroned on the mount of assembly. ... I will ascend above the tops of the clouds; I will make myself like the Most High.*
> **—Isaiah 14:13-14**

The devil decided to rebel out of a sense of ego and pride against the very God who created him. He saw the power that God possessed and wanted it for himself. Not surprisingly, God condemned his selfishness and banished him from heaven.

> *Your heart became proud on account of your beauty, and you corrupted your wisdom because of your splendor. So I threw you to the earth...*
> **—Ezekiel 28:17**

When he departed, Satan convinced a third of the angels in heaven to leave with him. These so-called "fallen angels" make up the corps of spectral minions that serve him today as demons.

Satan's primary goal on earth is to disparage the name of Jesus and wreak havoc in the lives of men. Pastor Chip Ingram explains in his book entitled, *The Invisible War*:

> *When scripture speaks of Satan, it isn't confined to small, passing comments or figures of speech. Satan is not a metaphor for evil. He is a powerful angel who committed treason against his Creator and convinced a third of the angels to rebel along with him. He now seeks to destroy all that is good and God ordained, and his strategy ever since his fall has been to tempt us with the same agenda he had—to be like God.*[92]

In simple terms, Satan will do anything in his power to separate us from God. And while he'll stop at nothing to accomplish his goals, he does not have the authority to control our lives.

Despite his status as a prominent angelic being, Satan is not an all-powerful entity. The devil is a "created being," and thus has limitations. He is not all-powerful, all-knowing, or ever-present on the earth like God. He can't make choices for you or read your mind. He can only observe your behavior and offer temptations that are consistent with what he sees.

Satan versus Job

More importantly, the devil cannot harm you without the expressed permission of God the Father. This principle is best illustrated in the very first chapter of the Book of Job. This story (perhaps the oldest written in the Bible) tells of a righteous man called Job from the land of Uz, a large area located east of the Jordan River Valley. The book begins with a brief description of Job and his family, as well as a summary of his cattle and livestock holdings. Then the narrative gets interesting:

> *One day the angels came to present themselves before the Lord,*
> *and Satan also came with them. The Lord said to Satan,*
> *'Where have you come from?' Satan answered the Lord,*
> *'From roaming throughout the earth, going back and forth*
> *on it.' Then the Lord said to Satan, 'Have you considered my*
> *servant Job? There is no one on earth like him; he is blameless*
> *and upright, a man who fears God and shuns evil.'*
> **—Job 1:6-8**

In looking at Job, Satan was decidedly unimpressed. He complained that Job was only a righteous man because he prospered and received God's favor. So he challenged God to take away all of Job's possessions, intending for him to curse the Lord in response.

> *The Lord said to Satan, 'Very well, then, everything he has*
> *is in your power, but on the man himself do not lay a finger.'*
> **—Job 1:12**

God accepted the devil's challenge by allowing him to have dominion over Job and his household. Satan attacked him with all his dark powers and eventually took away everything that he had. In spite of the devil's efforts to destroy him, Job refused to curse the Lord. His faith in God remained strong throughout the trials, and his family and fortunes were ultimately restored in the end. In fact, the Bible says that God blessed Job in the end with more than he had before the story began.

The main point to understand is that God has dominion over Satan at all times. Before he could destroy anything in Job's life or even touch a hair on his head, the devil had to obtain permission from the Lord. In Job's case, Satan was granted a divine endorsement, but God set limitations on what he could do. Remember: Satan was created by God, and is thereby subject to His authority. The devil may wish to destroy our lives, but his powers are limited by the Lord. In basic terms, God may allow the devil to tempt us on occasion, but He will always keep Satan on a short leash.

This is a critical point to reiterate; the devil cannot control your life unless you and God allow him to do so. As I've stated many times before, you alone control your choices and behavior. A silly excuse like, "The devil made me do it!" has no value in terms of theology or reality. In the case of substance abuse, when we run out of people to blame, we try to blame the substances themselves.

The Forbidden Fruit

The devil and his demonic henchmen primarily exist to destroy the lives of Christians and corrupt the name of Christ. The bad news is that they will use any tool (including intoxicating chemicals) at their disposal to achieve that end. In fact, I believe that drugs and alcohol are very much like the sinful fodder that Satan offered Adam and Eve in the Garden of Eden.

On some level, we all know that hallucinogenic substances are modern versions of the forbidden fruit. They are sinfully seductive in nature and offer the promise of godlike aspirations that mankind has come to crave. *When we ignore the commands of the Lord and take a bite, the devil deceives us into believing that this forbidden treat will transform us and our souls into the "gods of independence." In reality, a positive choice to abstain will result in the opposite reality—dependence on God.*

When the will of the Christian believer is in agreement with God's will, the devil's urgings can be resisted. James, the brother of Jesus, wrote:

> *Submit yourselves, then, to God. Resist the devil, and he will flee from you. Come near to God and he will come near to you.*
>
> **—James 4:7**

In this passage, we are commanded to "submit" ourselves to God and resist the dark forces in this world. This means that we need to place significant emphasis on controlling our thoughts, actions, and addictions.

The Holy Spirit was offered to help us accomplish these very goals. The Spirit of God works like a light within us to swallow up any darkness that is present. Jesus said:

> *See to it then, that the light within you is not darkness. Therefore if your whole body is full of light, and no part of it dark, it will be just as full of light as when a lamp shines its light on you.*
>
> **—Luke 11:35-36**

Remember, light always overcomes the darkness no matter how dense and black it may be. Light can exist in the darkest of places, but darkness must flee when it encounters the light. Jesus agreed:

> *The light shines in the darkness, and the darkness has not overcome it.*
>
> **—John 1:5**

Victory in Jesus

The best news of all is that while the devil is still fighting the battle, the war has already been won. When Jesus died on the cross, the devil was defeated once and for all. As we learned earlier, the devil is a created being and is thus under the authority of God and by extension Jesus and the Holy Spirit. *The blood of Jesus was the only blood necessarily spilled in this* war. *All we need to do is recognize this fact, and stop fighting a fight that has already been won!* By accepting the sacrifice, we are adopted as members of the winning team and are entitled to the benefits of Christian membership that include blessings, favor, and eternal life.

This doesn't mean that the devil has surrendered. He and his minions continue the fight with the ferocity of a caged lion. Their misguided perseverance reminds me of the first car I ever owned. It was a used Oldsmobile Cutlass Supreme built in the early 1980's. By the time I drove it the new car smell was long gone, but it ran well enough to get me where I needed to go. There was only one real problem with the car. When I turned off the key, the engine wouldn't always quit running. It would sputter, gasp, knock, and ping for several moments before finally dying.

This is what the devil is doing right now. The key has been turned off and the journey is over. The final destination has been determined and the ultimate goal of God to redeem mankind was achieved by Jesus Christ. Although the devil's fate has been decided, he is still launching his final attacks in a futile effort to tempt people to follow his lead. *Even though he cannot win, he is not yet willing to admit defeat. He'll sputter and gasp, knock and ping—but ultimately his end is inevitable.* As Paul wrote to the Church at Corinth:

> *When the perishable has been clothed with the imperishable, and the mortal with immortality, then the saying that was written will come true: Death has been swallowed up in victory.*
>
> **—I Corinthians 15:54**

CHAPTER NINETEEN

The Ultimate Cage Match: Flesh vs Spirit

For if you live according to the flesh, you will die; but if by the Spirit you put to death the misdeeds of the body, you will live.
—The Apostle Paul
Romans 8:13

G OD HAS GRANTED us salvation through his son Jesus so that we may spend eternity at His side. Although the sacrifice of Christ was not justified by our own behavior, we may attempt to make reparations to God by bringing our lives into alignment with His will. Remember: *Jesus took the punishment that we deserve.* In exchange, we Christians are expected to live in a way that exemplifies the character of God. Jesus stated this command clearly:

> *Do not love the world or anything in the world. If anyone loves the world, love for the Father is not in them. For everything in the world—the lust of the flesh, the lust of the eyes, and the pride of life—comes not from the Father but from the world. The world and its desires pass away, but whoever does the will of God lives forever.*
> **—John 2:15-17**

Assuming you have accepted Jesus and repented of your sins (including but not limited to chemical addictions), the question I would ask is simple. In your everyday life, how far are your "Saturday nights" from your "Sunday mornings?" How large of a gap exists between how you live and how God wishes for you to live? If you never spoke a word, would your life reflect the moral, ethical, and spiritual values of Christianity?

As we've discussed, the Bible indicates that the Holy Spirit lives within the hearts of believers. Along those lines, Paul wrote:

> *Do you not know that your bodies are temples of the Holy Spirit, who is in you, whom you have received from God? You are not your own; you were bought at a price. Therefore honor God with your bodies.*
>
> **—I Corinthians 6:19-20**

We must embrace the fact that we were "bought at a price" by the events that transpired at the cross. Therefore, our physical bodies have become the literal dwelling place of God. As a result, *God expects that we will honor this sacrifice by renovating our physical bodies into an acceptable residence for the Holy Spirit.*

Don't Trash God's Temple

This scripture boldly suggests that anyone responsible for doing damage to God's temple (our physical bodies) will be held responsible. Paul intended the previous passage to be a threat against self-destructive behavior. If we are to truly follow Christ, we must put aside our distractions, attractions, and addictions; not because we want to—but because we have to.

Along these lines, the Gospel of John tells the story of a disabled man who was sitting near a ritual pool in Jerusalem. The man had been paralyzed for thirty-eight years and was lying next to the water praying for a healing miracle. When Jesus learned of his condition, he immediately healed the man:

> *Then Jesus said to him, 'Get up! Pick up your mat and walk.'*
> *At once the man was cured; he picked up his mat and walked.*
>
> **—John 5:8-9**

This story is not all that different from the other healing miracles performed by Christ in the Gospels. However, this miracle is significant because of the words spoken by Jesus upon seeing the man later at the temple:

> *See, you are well again. Stop sinning or something worse may happen to you.*
>
> **—John 5:14**

After delivering the man from his paralytic condition, Jesus warned him to stop his sinful behavior. If he did not comply, there would be severe consequences. Something worse than his thirty-eight years of suffering might befall him. These must have been chilling words for the man to hear on the heels of his miraculous recovery.

Because we live in a sinful world, how can we possibly be expected to live without committing sins after we become Christians? The answer is fairly obvious—we cannot; but we are expected to try.

Flesh vs Spirit

Sin and obedience to God are polar opposites. Our tendency toward sin is often discussed in biblical terms as a desire to please the *flesh;* while the concept of obedience is described in terms of pleasing the *Spirit.* Our flesh is concerned mostly with the pleasures of this world, while the Holy Spirit within us focuses our attention on the principles of righteousness. These two are in a constant tug-of-war for dominance over us. Which one dominates your life?

Many people think about this struggle in terms of the popular images of angels and devils. Some people imagine that they have an angel sitting on one shoulder leading them down the path of righteousness. All the while, a devil is sitting on their other shoulder tempting you to give in to your primal urges and desires.

The angel represents the perfect will of God—manifested in the Spirit. The devil represents the desires of our flesh, such as our powerful longings for intoxication. The two are at odds with one another. Some people think that the one who most often wins is directing our everyday behavior. But if you are a believer and a follower of Christ, the devil has no power over you. You need to train yourself to listen to the Spirit more and the flesh less in order to avoid the potential for Godly correction down the road.

Another important thing to understand about an illustration like this is that people who abuse chemicals often labor under the delusion that the devilish options are the only options. Acting as though they are compelled to use substances, they don't even acknowledge the alternative of abstinence. They hear the voices of cravings and the desires of the flesh loud and clear. If you are a Christian and a substance abuser, you need to reverse this trend by giving the Spirit of God a dominant voice. When an unnatural desire to use chemicals arises, you need to turn up the volume of the Holy Spirit in order to avoid a move into the action phase of addiction.

Have you ever listened to music on headphones turned up so loud that you effectively drown out your surroundings? It's possible to become so engrossed in the music that you pay little or no attention to the rambunctious world around you. In terms of addiction, this is how we should listen to the voice of the Holy Spirit.

Spiritually speaking, ignoring a constant barrage of worldly thoughts by listening intently to the guidance of the Spirit is preferable and acceptable behavior. You cannot completely avoid this intruding noise, but you can drown it out until it fades into the background. In fact, the more often you listen and obey the voice of the Spirit of God, the less likely you will be to hear the discord of the devil. When you crank up the volume on your Holy Spirit headphones, you can learn to put to death the misdeeds of the body. The Apostle Paul states clearly:

> *So I say, walk by the Spirit, and you will not gratify the desires*
> *of the flesh. For the flesh desires what is contrary to the Spirit,*
> *and the Spirit what is contrary to the flesh. They are in conflict*
> *with each other, so that you are not to do whatever you want.*
> **—Galatians 5:16-17**

Who is Your Master?

In the Gospel of Matthew, Jesus began his public ministry near the Sea of Galilee, not far from his hometown of Nazareth. While he was in a town called Capernaum, he went up a mountainside to preach and teach. There he delivered what has become widely known as the Sermon on the Mount. He spoke that day on a number of subjects, but one in particular fits the context of our discussion on addiction.

> *No one can serve two masters. Either you will hate the one and love the other, or you will be devoted to the one and despise the other.*
>
> **—Matthew 6:24**

Jesus was saying that you can only be devoted to serving a singular part of your being. Devotion requires an intense focus on a single aspect of life, one that becomes identified as your "master." With these words, Jesus was likely alluding to the institution of slavery in antiquity.

When the Bible was written, slavery had evolved into a system that embodied absolute power, authority, and ownership. Most people born as slaves held unenviable positions in ancient society. They were considered the property of their masters and held no practical legal status of their own. Slaves and their families could even be passed down within a family from generation to generation as inherited property. As a result, one could remain in solemn servitude for a lifetime.

In terms of addiction, we've built a case that you are not a slave to your substance of choice. You are not required to obey the call of the chemicals because you have been endowed by your Creator with free will and the ability to choose sobriety. *In simple terms, we must consciously choose to serve God and nothing else.* The Apostle Paul wrote the following on the subject:

> *Don't you know that when you offer yourselves to someone as obedient slaves, you are slaves of the one you obey—whether you are slaves to sin, which leads to death, or to obedience, which leads to righteousness?*
>
> **—Romans 6:16**

In summation, the Bible identifies believers as the living, breathing temple of the Holy Spirit. As such, we are held to a higher standard of conduct for the remainder of our time on this earth. We are encouraged to cast aside the desires of the flesh and fully embrace the guidance of the Holy Spirit of God. Paul wrote:

> *Therefore, I urge you, brothers and sisters, in view of God's mercy, to offer your bodies as a living sacrifice, holy and pleasing to God—this is your true and proper worship. Do not conform to the pattern of this world, but be transformed by the renewing of your mind. Then you will be able to test and approve what God's will is—his good, pleasing and perfect will.*
>
> **—Romans 12:1-2**

CHAPTER TWENTY

Grace, Faith, and Indiana Jones

You will not have to fight this battle. Take up your positions;
stand firm and see the deliverance the Lord will give you.
—II Chronicles 20:17

OVER THE YEARS, I've been privileged to work with a lot of terrific people in the field of addiction. My duties on the staff of the Mississippi Drug Court have brought me into contact with a number of individuals who are attempting to "fight the good fight" against their chemical tendencies. I can honestly say that most of these people have a legitimate hunger for freedom and sobriety. While many are reluctant to admit the extent of their problems, they know that their lives have become unmanageable. It takes a great deal of courage to admit our weaknesses to others, especially when we know the probable reaction.

People are reluctant to be labeled as an "addict" even though their behavior more often than not merits the title. It's somewhat like being made to wear a T-shirt that says on the front, "I'm an addict!"—and on the back, "… and I don't deserve your respect." *But if you consider the truths of scripture, you'll realize that you are just being the sinner you were born to be.* In order to make a worthwhile change, you need to accept the transforming, redemptive power of Christ and become someone entirely different—a sinner saved by grace.

The biblical definition of grace is simple, yet astonishing. The word translated from the original Greek literally means "free gift."[93] So in terms of the Bible, we receive the blessings and favor of God although we've done absolutely nothing to deserve them. We cannot earn grace. We simply have to accept it as an unmerited gift from God. Paul wrote to Titus:

> *For the grace of God has appeared that offers salvation to all people. It teaches us to say 'No' to ungodliness and worldly passions, and to live self-controlled, upright and godly lives in this present age…*
>
> **—Titus 2:11-12**

According to these words, grace can teach us to lay aside our sins and earthly passions, including intoxicating substances. Some versions of the Bible use the phrase "deliverance from sin" in reference to these verses. In Greek, the word "deliverance" means "salvation."[94] The biblical use of this term means a "freedom from restraint or captivity." So in simple terms, deliverance is the immediate and miraculous freedom from sin.

Deliverance in the Bible

Mark recorded an incident in his Gospel that speaks on the subject of deliverance in a very interesting way. In the story, Jesus was traveling early in his ministry with his disciples near the Sea of Galilee. As he approached the shore, a large crowd began to follow him. Mark wrote:

> *And a woman was there who had been subject to bleeding for twelve years. She had suffered a great deal under the care of many doctors and had spent all she had, yet instead of getting better she grew worse.*
>
> **—Mark 5:25-26**

This woman probably suffered from some type of menstrual disorder. The story continues:

> *When she heard about Jesus, she came up behind him in the crowd and touched his cloak, because she thought, 'If I just touch his clothes, I will be healed.' Immediately her bleeding*

stopped and she felt in her body that she was free from her suffering.

—Mark 5:27-29

When she touched his garment, Jesus realized that "power" had been drawn from him. He then asked his disciples who touched him. The disciples thought this was a silly question because the people in the crowd were pressing against him on all sides. Nevertheless, Jesus continued to search for the person who had "touched" him.

Then the woman, knowing what had happened to her, came and fell at his feet and, trembling with fear, told him the whole truth. He said to her, 'Daughter, your faith has healed you. Go in peace and be freed from your suffering.'

—Mark 5:33-34

There are a number of important things we can learn from this story. First of all, we need to understand the gravity of the woman's situation. The Bible says that she suffered bleeding like this for twelve years. She must have had a wretched existence, but not just because of her health issues. The Law of Moses (given in the Old Testament Book of Leviticus) stated that no Jew was allowed to have any contact with a woman suffering from extensive blood loss. As a result, this woman would likely have been shunned by everyone around her. She would have been avoided by people at all costs in order that they might keep from becoming "ceremonially unclean."

The passage also states that the woman suffered under the care of many doctors, having spent all of her resources on false cures. Sound familiar? Over the years, I've known numerous people who have been in and out of addiction treatment facilities. They've been fed the principles of disease theory with such regularity that they feel helpless and are often unwilling to make additional attempts at rehabilitation. Many families have been ruined financially by the fiscal burden of recovery programs, despite the fact that they have seen little or no improvement in their loved ones' behavior.

According to Mark, the woman in question exhibited an enviable amount of faith in the restorative powers of Jesus. She felt that if she could only "touch his clothes" she would be healed. Her faith is remarkable considering the fact that Jesus hadn't yet been identified publicly as the Messiah. He was simply a local Jewish teacher who supposedly had miraculous powers. Nevertheless, she had likely heard of his teachings and knew about some of the miracles he had performed in the name of God.

The passage states that Jesus felt that "power had gone out from him" when he was touched. He knew that someone had reached out to him and taken healing power. The disciples probably thought he was crazy when he asked who had touched him, considering the size and proximity of the crowd. Regardless, Jesus needed to find the woman to confirm that she had been healed and also to publicly commend her faith. When the woman realized she was well, she fell at his feet and proceeded to tell him the "whole truth."

Have you ever taken the time to tell Jesus the "whole truth?" Have you totally humbled yourself and confessed all the sin that exists in your life? Even though God already knows the extent of it all, He wants to hear it from you.

Confession and the Lord

My wife Melissa and I have been blessed with two children, a boy and a girl. They are fraternal twins who were born about three minutes apart. Generally speaking, they are well behaved kids and they both love the Lord. But when they were young, they were not always well behaved. My wife or I would eventually find the evidence of their misdeeds and put together the pieces of the puzzle in order to identify the guilty party. Most of the time, we knew "who had done what" before we asked, but we still wanted to hear the truth from them.

That's the way God treats us sometimes. As our Father, He knows that we will be disobedient and He definitely knows that we will try to hide the evidence of the crime. He doesn't necessarily punish us for this, but He may discipline us over time if we never confess the truth. The word for *confess* in the New Testament Greek means "to admit or acknowledge something to another."[95]

Most people evade the label of an addict to avoid the judgment of others. They want the benefits that come with intoxication, but they want little to do with the costs. They often pull away from family and friends out of a sense of shame or remorse. They effectively go into hiding and become fully enveloped in a persistent state of intoxication.

By the time you publicly acknowledge your substance abuse, your "secret" has probably been out for a while. The people in your life know more than you think, having witnessed the destruction first hand. When you finally admit your addictive issues, your friends and family are well aware of your guilt.

Typically, confession implies an active desire by the guilty party to acknowledge their deeds before they are ever presumed guilty. A defendant may admit guilt in a court of law, but a confession of that guilt beforehand may result in avoiding court altogether.

Confession is what God desires from us. He wants us to willingly acknowledge our faults before Him—with no court appearance necessary. Confession is often accompanied by a degree of absolution. In the eyes of God, we are granted a pardon and complete forgiveness at the time of confession.

The Apostle John wrote:

> *If we claim to be without sin, we deceive ourselves and the truth is not in us. If we confess our sins, he is faithful and just and will forgive us our sins and purify us from all unrighteousness.*
>
> **—I John 1:8-9**

Now is a good time to approach God and unburden your heart by telling the "whole truth" about your substance abuse. The burden of guilt is then lifted. No plea bargain is necessary ... forgiveness is guaranteed!

What is Faith?

When Jesus told the woman that her "faith" had healed her, he meant that she had been delivered from her affliction because she believed in his healing powers. Do you believe in the power of faith? The writer of the

Book of Hebrews in the New Testament gave us a biblical definition of "faith."

> *Now faith is confidence in what we hope for and assurance*
> *about what we do not see.*
>
> **—Hebrews 11:1**

This definition indicates a willingness to ask without fear and hesitation for certain gifts or favors from God. If we have faith, we can boldly submit our requests in the form of prayers and expect to have them granted. Jesus told his followers:

> *You may ask me for anything in my name, and I will do it.*
>
> **—John 14:14**

The second part of this definition of faith gives us "assurance" that God exists and provides for us even though we cannot see Him. Remember the story of Elisha and his servant from the Old Testament? That story tells us that there are supernatural events taking place around us every day. It is important to acknowledge this fact in order to exercise the workings of our faith. We must believe in the reality of the power and presence of the Trinity: God the Father, God the Son, and God the Holy Spirit. Yet, we must also be aware of the opposing negative forces at work under the direction of Satan. Even though we have the assurance from God that Satan's powers are limited, we must be vigilant in resisting his dark influence.

When I think of the concept of faith, I am reminded of a particular scene in a popular movie from the 1980's. In the film *Indiana Jones and the Last Crusade,* the title character was on a quest to find the Holy Grail, which was believed to have been the cup used by Jesus at the Last Supper. Throughout the film, Harrison Ford's character was faced with a series of obstacles as he sought to save the life of his father and pursue the grail of Christ. As the movie reached its climax, he was presented with a daunting task. He found himself on the edge of a large ravine which he needed to cross to enter the chamber containing the holy relic. However, attempts to do so appeared impossible to accomplish through his physical abilities alone.

Having been instructed to have "faith in God" to traverse the distance, he had to reassess the situation. He made the decision to close his eyes and step out into the void based on the premise and the promise of faith. When he stepped into the unknown, his foot landed on solid ground in the form of an invisible bridge. It was imperceptible to the human eye, but it existed across the divide all along. He wasn't aware of its existence until he stepped out in faith, trusting God to provide a solution to the problem. In the movie, he then proceeded across this bridge to once again save the day.

In life, we are sometimes faced with seemingly insurmountable obstacles (like substance abuse), and we often have no idea how to overcome them. We look at the gap that exists between where we are and where we want to be with the very same skepticism. Since we are not physically capable of leaping the distance under our own power, we think, "How in the world can I cross that divide?" As a result, we can become discouraged and surrender to an overwhelming feeling of powerlessness.

Fortunately, God has already provided a "bridge" to enable us to avoid the fall. We simply need to have the guts to step out in faith and believe it will support our weight. God knew all along that we would create situations in our lives that would require it, so He placed it in our paths long ago. *You need only to believe with all of your heart that it exists.* Undoubtedly, this "bridge of faith" will hold the weight of your problems and lead you successfully to your destination of freedom from those issues.

Spiritual Deliverance Is Real and Possible

If you cultivate your faith, you can be delivered from your addictions in an immediate and supernatural way. I've seen many people delivered from substance abuse through faith and the power of prayer. These divine healings are not uncommon, and they have profound transformative effects on the people they bless. Jesus confirmed that fact:

> *With man this is impossible, but with God all things are possible.*
> **—Matthew 19:26**

The late Dr. Gerald May was a well-known physician and psychiatrist in the addiction industry for more than 25 years. He counseled many patients over the course of his career and was no stranger to the concept of divine intervention. Dr. May wrote:

> *I identified a few people who seemed to have overcome serious addictions to alcohol and other drugs, and I asked them what had helped them turn their lives around so dramatically ... They kindly acknowledged their appreciation for the professional help they had received, but they also made it clear that this help had not been the source of their healing. What had healed them was something spiritual. It had something to do with turning to God.*[96]

Over the years, Dr. May witnessed numerous real world instances of these kinds of miraculous healings. He described the phenomena as follows:

> *I can only call it deliverance. There is no physical, psychological, or social explanation for such hidden empowerments. People who have experienced them call them miraculous. In many cases, these people have struggled with their addictions for years. Then suddenly, with no warning, the power of addiction is broken.*[97]

The question is—"What are you afraid of?" Are you afraid to ask God for deliverance from your addictions because you fear that he may not answer your prayers? Do you think you're not good enough or spiritual enough to warrant God's assistance? Or do you think you don't have enough faith? Jesus stated quite clearly:

> *Therefore I tell you, whatever you ask for in prayer, believe that you have received it, and it will be yours.*
> **—Mark 11:24**

Fear is the opposite of faith. It is the cat to our dog, the hot to our cold, and eventually the hell to our heaven. In fact, the late great pastor Kenneth Hagin said simply, "Fear is faith in the devil." Are you afraid to admit a stubborn reluctance to release your grip on the forbidden fruit? Or are you afraid—not that God won't answer your prayers—but that He will?

The changes in my brother were evident, and not just externally. As Kevin took the necessary steps to regain control of his life, his physical appearance changed. He no longer had the shallow look of an "addict." More remarkably, a major internal transformation had begun. It was a gradual alteration of sorts that required determination and perseverance as he reevaluated his priorities. He eventually became more self-aware in order to recognize the "triggers" (people, places, and activities) that might contribute to a relapse. His recovery was by no means perfect, but drugs no longer controlled his life. He struggled initially with cravings, but he was able to bring them into submission with the ever-present help of the Holy Spirit.

As he matured into his late twenties, Kevin started to question the validity of the disease concept of addiction. Without a doubt, he made it clear to me that one of the most important steps in his recovery involved accepting personal responsibility for his actions. "I did it to myself," he said. "I made those choices and now I have to live with them."

Kevin entered addiction treatment for a final time in 2001. This faith-based facility offered a curriculum that was a perfect fit for that particular stage in his recovery. While in treatment, he was introduced to a beautiful young woman named Roma. They seemed made for each other from the very beginning. When they completed treatment, they started dating, supporting each other in their recoveries. They eventually got engaged to be married and worked together in a retail location of our family business.

Their first child, Sean Michael Mason, was born on October 4, 2002. I vividly recall my first visit with them just a few days after his birth. When I held Sean in my arms for the very first time, it brought back memories of the first time I held my baby brother. The joy of that moment will not soon be forgotten. A few weeks later, I received a phone call at my office from a tired, yet exuberant new father. Kevin was exhausted, but at the same time elated about the blessings of this new-found gift. We talked about how different things can be when we make choices that are in agreement with the will of God. Before he hung up, Kevin said, "These last few weeks have been the happiest times of my life!" After all he had been through, I knew exactly what he meant.

CHAPTER TWENTY-ONE

Opportunity Knocks but Temptation Leans on the Doorbell

When tempted, no one should say, "God is tempting me." For God cannot be tempted by evil, nor does he tempt anyone; but each person is tempted when they are dragged away by their own evil desire and enticed. Then, after desire has conceived, it gives birth to sin; and sin, when it is full-grown, gives birth to death.

—James (Brother of Jesus)
James 1:13

A T THIS POINT, we need to discuss the various phenomena singularly associated with addiction as sin in our lives. If we understand the message of the Bible as it relates to certain aspects of addictive behaviors, we can attempt to derail them before they can take control of our lives. Anyone whose been trained in the techniques of combat will respond instinctively during battle. The same is true for those of us who actively work to overcome dependent behaviors.

Let's begin with the concept of cravings, which are an influential component in determining our chemical behaviors. According to disease theory, a craving is a "compulsive urge that has been created in the brain and is manifested physically."[98]

As a so-called "compulsive urge," these cravings are thought to drive impulsive actions that are almost impossible to resist. This is the definition of cravings that has been driven home for decades by disease theory proponents. As it turns out, the words "almost impossible" are more significant than we've been led to believe. Consider the following words written by disease theory apologist Dr. Harold Urschel:

> *While it's true that you cannot prevent cravings from arising, you can control whether you will respond by drinking or using. The startling fact is people in recovery typically give in to only about 5% of their cravings!*[99]

Take a moment to let this sink in. This is a really important point to comprehend. *One of the most well-respected physicians in the field of addiction studies confirms the fact that you have the absolute ability to control your response to cravings for intoxicating substances.* In fact, Dr. Urschel admits that the average person in the process of recovery succumbs to only 5 out of 100 cravings. Do these results seem consistent with the theory of addiction is a disease?

Harvard research psychologist Gene Heyman takes this idea one step further:

> *If most addicts quit and cravings are common, then millions of addicts must have experienced cravings to resume drug use but learned how not to give in to them. Thus cravings are not a sufficient condition for drug use; they do not make it obligatory.*[100]

In other words, it's not possible to blame persistent chemical abuse on the simple existence of cravings. Their very definition implies that they are nearly impossible to ignore, but real world research seem to support the opposite conclusion. People can—and do—resist cravings for drugs and alcohol every single day. *No matter what you've been told, cravings do not require an active response.*

It is essential that you understand this one simple point. The thought of using (which is often identified as a craving) is not the same as the active response required to ingest intoxicating chemicals. Just because you've had the thought does not mean that you are required to act on it.

As stated earlier, God created each of us with the gift of free will in our lives. Ultimately, this means that we alone control our response… not some chemical compound.

Establishing Authority over Cravings

People throughout history have discovered how to take certain natural elements (like opium) and synthesize them into substances that create feelings of euphoric pleasure. This is how mankind created intoxicating chemicals like drugs and alcohol. Along those same lines, we have already learned that God created Satan and thus has authority over him. In much the same way, mankind needs to recognize and exert our own authority over the very intoxicating compounds that we ourselves created. *In the same way that God has authority over the devil, believers have authority over drugs and alcohol. We control them; they do not control us.* If they control you, then you have elevated them to the status of gods, and they will certainly not hesitate to accept your sacrifices.

However, if you can establish ultimate authority over them and bring your thoughts under control, you may well have the ammunition necessary to win each battle and eventually the war as a whole. This simple concept is reinforced by addiction specialist Dr. Harold Urschel:

> *If you continually resist the urge to drink or use when exposed to a trigger, your body and the hippocampal system in your brain will come to understand that the trigger is not a sign of good things to come. The dopamine system will no longer be automatically activated and eventually the trigger will fail to produce a craving. That's why cravings become weaker the longer you stay sober.*[101]

If you can resist the first craving, you've won the initial battle and begun to separate the thought from the action. The more often these battles are won, the more separation there will be between the cravings and their active responses.

I once heard someone say, "Your mind is like a bad neighborhood— don't go there alone!" With the powerful presence of the Holy Spirit, you'll never have to go it alone! Remember: One of the Holy Spirit's primary functions is to convict us of our sins and direct us toward selflessness. If you've been *born again*, the indwelt Spirit of God will instruct you to make responsible choices with regard to these cravings. This practice of repetitive resistance will help you to take the necessary steps toward sobriety.

Temptation in the Bible

Although cravings are not mentioned by name in the Bible, the general concept is addressed in terms of temptation. The word for "temptation" in the Greek is "peirasmos," which means literally a "test or trial."[102] In my view, "tests" do not come directly from God because He is already aware of the condition of our hearts and minds. Instead, these emotional exams show us who we really are and who we wish to be. Temptation can teach us things about ourselves that we may not even want to know.

While the devil is often known in scripture as the "Tempter," he and his cohorts are not always responsible for the endless temptations that we face. For instance, if you have a problem with drinking, you cannot blame Satan if you find yourself strolling through a liquor store. If you have a problem with painkillers, you shouldn't blame a continued association with a drug dealer on the influence of demonic powers. As stated clearly in our Common Sense Model (CSM) of addition, you are responsible for the quality of your own choices, and your environment is crucial in terms of seeking or skirting sobriety. On this subject, Paul wrote:

> *Do not be yoked together with unbelievers. For what do righteousness and wickedness have in common? Or what fellowship can light have with the darkness?*
> **—II Corinthians 6:14**

If you recall the depiction of Jesus' preparation to begin his public ministry, he was tempted for forty straight days in the wilderness. He went without food, water, and companionship for that time. He was tempted three times by the devil himself, but he emerged victorious to continue his ministry. It is for this very reason that we may trust in Jesus to strengthen us during times of trouble:

> *Because he himself suffered when he was tempted, he is able*
> *to help those who are being tempted.*
>
> **—Hebrews 2:18**

Although Jesus understood that we are inherently susceptible, he warned us against falling into temptations of any kind. We need to stand strong against the stubborn desires of the flesh:

> *Watch and pray so that you will not fall into temptation. The*
> *Spirit is willing, but the flesh is weak.*
>
> **—Mark 14:38**

We need to actively discourage those fleshly thoughts and set our minds on the things of God. On the subject, the Apostle Paul told the churchgoers at Philippi:

> *Finally, brothers and sisters, whatever is true, whatever*
> *is noble, whatever is right, whatever is pure, whatever is*
> *lovely, whatever is admirable—if anything is excellent or*
> *praiseworthy—think about such things.*
>
> **—Philippians 4:8**

It's important to understand that the Holy Spirit and the old nature that we cast aside upon our salvation are on opposite sides in a spiritual tug-of-war. Often our old self presents a problem because it keeps a firm grasp on the rope. While trying to regain ownership of our souls, it will pull on that rope until it comes to the realization that the Spirit cannot be defeated.

Taking Your Thoughts Captive

Paul also told the church at Corinth that we are fighting a war in our minds for control of our innermost thoughts:

> *The weapons we fight with are not the weapons of the*
> *world. On the contrary, they have divine power to demolish*

strongholds. We demolish arguments and every pretension that sets itself up against the knowledge of God, and we take captive every thought to make it obedient to Christ.

—II Corinthians 10:4-5

This is one of my favorite passages in the New Testament. It encourages us to fight the battle for our very own souls by embracing the divine powers granted us as believers in God. We can demolish the stubborn "strongholds" of our addictions and persistent preoccupations with intoxicating chemicals. If we can learn to change our states of mind and redirect our thoughts in ways that promote responsible choices, we can break free from the captivity of substance abuse and experience the freedom of sustained sobriety.

There is one final point on this subject that addicts need to understand. *In spite of the nature of your current situation, the Lord will never give you more temptation than you can handle.* Paul wrote these words to the early followers of Christ in Corinth:

No temptation has overtaken you except what is common to mankind. And God is faithful; he will not let you be tempted beyond what you can bear. But when you are tempted, he will also provide a way out so that you can endure it.

—I Corinthians 10:13

Paul said that you will face temptations everyday that are not uncommon to others. He stressed that God is ever faithful, and will never allow you to be tempted beyond your capacity to withstand. When you are in the midst of a seemingly impossible cycle of provocations, remember that God will always provide a means of escape!!!

CHAPTER TWENTY-TWO

Your Final Decision Brings Final Judgment!

I have told you these things so that in me you may have peace. In this world you will have trouble. But take heart! I have overcome the world.

—Jesus Christ
John 16:33

THE WORLD WE live in is messy to say the least. It's almost as though God gave mankind a blank canvas and gives everyone an opportunity to paint. The problem is, instead of using brushes, we tend to use our hands and the resulting images look like the work of seven billion finger-painting toddlers. The real problem with finger painting is that it's a messy process, which often results in mankind being completely covered in the colors of chaos and catastrophe. Even those people who try their best to stay clean seem to have limited success in doing so.

Life is hard sometimes, and we're often left to wonder, "Why?" Some of us are stained by our own colors, resulting in images that are not pleasing to the eye. However, when we are inadvertently splattered by the work of other artists, we have more difficulty appreciating the end results. This is one of the hardest things to reconcile with God.

Why do bad things happen to good people? Nobody really knows because the God who created the universe is in charge of that department, and He doesn't really owe us an explanation. This belief is echoed in the Book of Job:

> *Can you fathom the mysteries of God? Can you probe the*
> *limits of the Almighty? They are higher than the heavens*
> *above—what can you do? They are deeper than the depths*
> *below—what can you know?*
>
> **—Job 11:7-8**

The bottom line is this: Our task on earth is not to understand why things happen, but to learn to deal with them when they do. The trials of life are not thrust upon us so that God can test our inner strength. He has no need to challenge us for His enlightenment. Maybe certain obstacles are placed in our paths so that we can discover our true capabilities as believers.

This reminds me of the process of working out our bodies by lifting weights. When we go through a rigorous workout that involves some form of weight training, we put our bodies under a certain degree of stress. When we strain our muscles to their limits, we are actually tearing them down on a microscopic level. After the workout, our muscles begin to repair themselves if we are properly nourished. Over time they become stronger and muscle mass increases.

The Furnace of Affliction

In this way, God puts us through workouts so that we can gain in strength, wisdom, and faith. The real problem is that we don't have the option of skipping a workout because we don't feel well or are just plain lazy. Like it or not, God will put you through a workout to ultimately make you stronger. The Lord confirms this idea through the words of the prophet Isaiah:

> *See, I have refined you, though not as silver; I have tested you*
> *in the furnace of affliction.*
>
> **—Isaiah 48:10**

This scripture makes reference to the antique practice of refining silver, which is a process that has changed very little in thousands of years. The raw metal is placed in a crucible and inserted into a furnace to be heated. As the metal encounters the heat, it is purged of imperfections and the natural impurities begin to separate from the body of the metal, itself. In this way, the silver is purified and ready to be formed into something useful. Most importantly, the silversmith has to watch over the liquefied mix for the entire time that it is exposed to the heat. If the silver stays in the fire for even a moment too long, it can be destroyed. In much the same way, God watches over us as we endure the fiery trials of life. He keeps a close eye out to ensure that we don't remain in the furnace for too long.

Do you sometimes feel like you have been in the fire for way too long? Does your life seem like nothing more than a series of fiery episodes punctuated by brief respites from the heat? If so, the good news is that God must have very specific plans for you, because higher temperatures produce higher quality results. In fact, some of the most precious metals in the world (including gold) are refined at the highest temperatures. In recognition of this fact, the much maligned Job declared:

> *But he (God) knows the way that I take; when he has tested me, I will come forth as gold.*
>
> **—Job 23:10**

My friend Wade Carey has written a number Christian books of fiction that mix scripture with sound biblical principles. Most of his novels revolve around the adventures of an affable angel named Mick, who is tasked with fighting demons in the midst of the larger spiritual war. In his book entitled, *A Walk Through the Mall,* the angel Mick offered the following thoughts on the subject of trials and tribulations:

> *Think of the tribulations in your life as if they were raindrops landing on your windshield, trying to distract you from seeing past them at the road in front of you. Although you utilize your wipers to wipe them away, you ultimately become accustomed to the rain coming down, and your wipers moving across your windshield. Essentially it becomes second nature to you. ... The wipers represent the Bible, and the Bible points to Christ. When you learn to trust the Word of God, you won't be distracted by Satan's thunderstorms of trouble.*[103]

Unfortunately, we now understand that we can do little (on our own) to stop the stains of life from covering us. We've also learned that God will often place us in a *furnace of affliction* in order to refine us and strengthen our resolve. Now, if we learn to look to the Bible for encouragement in the midst of our troubles, the storms of the devil will never distort our view.

The Apostle Paul certainly knew all about the heat that often comes with earnestly living for God. Over the course of his ministry, Paul was beaten regularly and nearly stoned to death for speaking out in faith. He survived three shipwrecks, and was imprisoned by the Romans for more than five years. If anyone (other than Jesus) ever had a reason to complain, it might be the Apostle Paul. Nevertheless, he wrote the following:

> *Who shall separate us from the love of Christ? Shall trouble or hardship or persecution or famine or nakedness or danger or sword? As it is written:'For your sake we face death all day long: we are considered as sheep to be slaughtered.' No, in all these things we are more than conquerors through him who loved us. For I am convinced that neither death nor life, neither angels nor demons, neither the present nor the future, nor any powers, neither height nor depth, nor anything else in all creation, will be able to separate us from the love of God that is in Christ Jesus our Lord.*
>
> **—Romans 8:35-39**

Paul said that we can become "more than conquerors" over earthly distractions through the power afforded us by our relationship with Christ. In spite of the overwhelming heat, he never let the weight of life crush his spirit. Paul refused to let these obstacles impede his walk, and he even rejoiced in them as stripes earned in service to the Lord.

Final Judgment in the Bible

God the Father commands us to cast aside the cares of this world and offer our very lives in service to His kingdom. If we choose not to do so, we will undoubtedly face the consequences. It is important for you to understand one specific event that will definitely occur at the end of the world. The Apostle Paul wrote:

> *For we must all appear before the judgment seat of Christ, so*
> *that each of us may receive what is due us for the things done*
> *while in the body, whether good or bad.*
> **—II Corinthians 5:10**

If you believe that God exists and that heaven and hell are real, then you should also believe that mankind will be judged at the end of this current age. This is not an abstract idea that comes from some obscure book from antiquity, but a real event that will take place whether you're ready for it or not.

The entire Book of Revelation gives us a God-inspired account of the events that will come to pass in the last days. The writer of this Book (likely the Apostle John) wrote about a vision he experienced concerning the end of the world:

> *And I saw the dead standing, great and small, standing*
> *before the throne, and books were opened. Another book*
> *was opened, which is the book of life. The dead were judged*
> *according to what they had done as recorded in the books. ...*
> *Anyone whose name was not found written in the book of life*
> *was thrown into the lake of fire.*
> **—Revelation 20:12-15**

Here's the bottom line: When the time comes, God won't ask whether or not you are prepared to leave this earth; He'll simply make it happen. And when He does, the question becomes: *Will your name be written in the "book of life?"*

Right or Left ... Heaven or Hell?

One final story from the Bible explains the salvation decision in its most basic form. According to the Gospels, when Jesus was led out to be crucified, he was executed alongside two criminals—one on his left and one on his right. We know that the three men were nailed to their crosses and placed upright on the hill called Golgotha. Scripture tells us that many people witnessed this event and shouted insults at Christ as he hung on the cross. Luke then wrote:

> *One of the criminals who hung there hurled insults at him: 'Aren't you the Messiah? Save yourself and us!' But the other criminal rebuked him. 'Don't you fear God,' he said, 'since you are under the same sentence? We are punished justly, for we are getting what we deserve. But this man has done nothing wrong.'*
>
> **—Luke 23:39-41**

This scene represents the situation that all mankind will face as we look death and judgment in the eye. Luke wrote only that the two other men were "criminals," so we don't know exactly what they did to earn their fates. Nevertheless, they hung helplessly alongside Jesus awaiting the end of their time on earth. For the purposes of this discussion, I imagine the criminal on the left to be the one who mocked Jesus and questioned his divine calling. This man seemed resigned to his fate and exhibited no feelings of repentance or remorse.

On the other hand, the criminal on the right observed the mockery of Jesus and found it inappropriate and detestable. He defended Jesus by rebuking the other man and asking him sternly, "Don't you fear God?" The man on the right (according to my imagination) admitted that his behavior warranted punishment, and that he deserved to be crucified. He stated correctly that Jesus had done nothing to deserve his fate, and he humbly recognized the divinity of Christ.

In this life, we all deserve to hang on a cross for living in direct opposition to the will of God. In this story, both men were condemned to die as a result of worshiping their own gods of sin and indulgence. Admittedly, we are no different. You and I could just as easily be hanging alongside Jesus on that hill, dying the slow, agonizing death of crucifixion. Based on this imagination of the criminals on the cross, one question remains. *"Where do you stand with Jesus Christ—on the left or the right side?"*

If you hang to the left, you are not yet ready to admit your faults and accept his forgiveness. You choose deliberate disobedience and mockery over healing and deliverance. You choose substances over sobriety, yourself over God, and ultimately hell over heaven.

If you hang on the right, you've reached a turning point in your life. You recognize your sins and deliberately repent of your colored past. You realize that Jesus took the punishment that you deserve, and you're ready to be redeemed. All you need to do is accept the love of Christ and humbly ask for forgiveness.

The biblical account continues after the man on the right criticized the other criminal for his lack of faith and compassion. The penitent criminal then made the following request:

> *Jesus, remember me when you come into your kingdom.*
> —**Luke 23:42**

Luke then ends the story with Jesus speaking some of the sweetest words ever recorded:

> *Jesus answered him, 'Truly I tell you, today you will be with me in paradise.'*
> —**Luke 23:43**

Take A Stand

It's important for us to understand one final, critical point. Jesus stated clearly that we are required to make an active choice:

> *Whoever believes in the Son has eternal life, but whoever rejects the Son will not see life, for God's wrath remains on them.*
> —**John 3:36**

These words are solemn and unambiguous. In this life, there are choices to be made: addiction or sobriety; sin or salvation; hell or heaven. *Without a doubt, you have the right to deliberately refuse to follow God. But if you choose a life of independence over a life dependent on God, be prepared to face the consequences.* Jesus said plainly:

> *Whoever is not with me is against me, and whoever does not gather with me scatters.*
>
> **—Matthew 12:30**

These words were spoken after Christ drove a demon out of a possessed man. He was fresh from a real life battle in the larger spiritual war against the devil. Like it or not, you now find yourself engaged on a similar battlefield. For your sake, I urge you not to wait until it's too late to choose sides with God. C.S. Lewis wrote:

> *Never fear. There are only two kinds of people in the end: those who say to God, 'Thy <u>will</u> be done,' and those to whom God says, in the end, '<u>Thy</u> will be done.' All that are in hell choose it.*[104]

Remember—if you choose not to make a decision, you have still made a choice. Like it or not, you will have taken a deliberate stance in opposition to God. The consequences of not recognizing God's authority and/or deciding not to follow Him are one in the same:

> *He will punish those who do not know God and do not obey the Gospel of our Lord Jesus. They will be punished with everlasting destruction and shut out from the presence of the Lord and from the glory of his might.*
>
> **—II Thessalonians 1:8-9**

Fortunately, the best news of all is that you still have an opportunity to reconcile yourself to God through Jesus Christ. It took only a few seconds for the penitent criminal to ask Jesus for the keys to the kingdom of heaven. The same can be true for you.

What is Your Final Answer?

Robert "Evel" Knievel gave his final answer on April 1st, 2007. He explained that something happened to him on that day in a motel room in Daytona Beach, Florida. Having lived a turbulent life defined by selfish choices, he made a sudden decision that would change his prospects for eternity. He described the event that caused him to "wake up" in a television interview later that year.

> *"I said, 'Devil, Devil, get away from me... I cast you out of my life...You will be gone, I don't want you around me anymore.' I did everything I could. I put my knees on the ground. I prayed that God would put His arms around me and never let me go."*

My childhood hero decided to turn away from his "wild living" and turn toward Christ. He died of lung disease less than eight months later.

Where do you stand in relation to God? Have you made your choice? The author of the Book of Hebrews wrote:

> *God again set a certain day, calling it 'today.' 'Today if you hear his voice do not harden your hearts.'*
> **—Hebrews 4:7**

Make today the most important day of your life by praying a solemn, quiet prayer for salvation through Christ. If you don't know what to say, I have included a simple prayer at the end of this book.

If you've already done so, you have undoubtedly made the most important decision of all. Although your life will still be filled with obstacles big and small, you will never again have to navigate them alone. When you find yourself headed into dangerous waters, let the Holy Spirit take the wheel and your spiritual journey through addiction will have a truly happy ending.

The prophet Jeremiah wrote the following words nearly 3,000 years ago, but they still echo with truth today:

'For I know the plans I have for you,' declares the Lord, 'plans to prosper you and not to harm you, plans to give you hope and a future.'

—Jeremiah 29:11

God has loved you since the beginning of time, and that will never change. He wants you to prosper in life, as you will in death in His name. To do so, you need to set aside your selfish, sinful addictions in order to receive His many blessings. When you accomplish this in spiritual terms, you can boldly proclaim the transcendent relationship between addiction and God.

The phone rang just after midnight on Thursday, November 15, 2002—which is never a good sign. My Mother was on the line sobbing, "Kevin's gone! Kevin's gone! Kevin's gone!" At first, I didn't understand. Gone where? Then the reality of her words and the gravity of her tone struck me like a bolt of lightning. I was suddenly enveloped in a fog of emotional hysteria—one that would not soon dissipate.

Kevin, my only brother, was indeed gone from this world. Since he had not returned home from work at the usual hour, my Mother drove to our store assuming that he was having car trouble. When she reached the store, she found his lifeless body inside. Kevin had been diagnosed several years earlier with a blood disorder that caused chronic problems with clots in his legs and body. One of these dangerous clots had formed and traveled to his heart, resulting in his sudden, untimely death.

I was paralyzed with grief, but I quickly recovered my senses and was determined to be strong for my family. My parents and his fiance were understandably devastated. I drove through the night to be with them... all the while trying to gather the pieces of my own shattered consciousness. I had to come to grips with the fact that I had lost my only brother ... and my newborn nephew had lost his father.

The pain of that day still lingers and the scars will forever remain. But we as a family have persevered, making that difficult journey through the furnace of affliction. Since Kevin's death, our family and my faith have grown exponentially. Kevin's son, Sean Michael Mason, has grown into a healthy and happy young man with a familiar gleam in his eye. Although I don't get to see him as often as I'd like, his every smile reminds me of his father.

To many, this may seem like a somber ending to Kevin's story—but I respectfully disagree. My brother, my confidant, and my best friend may be gone from this earth, but he will always be a part of my life. "Gone where?"—you might ask. The answer is obvious; he's gone to heaven! He was lost but has been found; he was dead but his soul lives again in Christ. Without a moments doubt, I know that I'll see him again someday. And when I do, it will be just as joyous as the first time I ever laid eyes on him!

EPILOGUE

This is not the end, nor is it the beginning of the end. But perhaps it is the end of the beginning.
—Sir Winston Churchill

THE FOLLOWING IS an example of a simple prayer of salvation. If you voice these words with passion and sincerity, your prayers will be answered and you'll be *born again*. You may wish to pray to God in your own words, which may seem more natural to you. In the end, the words matter less than the desire of your heart.

> *Father God, as I sit here alone in the shadow of my sins, I realize that I've been running away from you all my life. I understand that I was born into a fallen world and have been living a life of sin and selfishness all along. I know that I've pushed you away by choosing to worship myself (and chemicals) instead of you. I want to turn away from the desires of my former life and the darkness within me that stains my soul.*

> *I surrender my life to your son Jesus. I believe that He lived a sinless life and died a sinner's death on the cross. I understand that he offered Himself as a sacrifice for every one of my sins, including those related to addiction. I believe that He was resurrected and ascended to heaven, having paid the debt that I owed for my plentiful personal sins.*

Please help me to conquer my addictive behaviors with the power and presence of your Holy Spirit. Give me a humble heart and encourage me so that I may serve as an example to others. And finally, grant me the joy and miraculous peace of salvation in Jesus Christ.

—Amen

NOTES

1   Harold C. Urschell, III, MD, <u>Healing the Addicted Brain</u> (Naperville, IL: Sourcebooks, Inc, 2009) p.6.

2   Gene M. Heyman, <u>Addiction: A Disorder of Choice</u> (Cambridge, MA: Harvard University Press, 2009) p.14.

3   Gene M. Heyman, <u>Addiction: A Disorder of Choice</u> (Cambridge, MA: Harvard University Press, 2009) p.65.

4   "addiction." Merriam-Webster.com. Merriam-Webster, 2012. (July 2, 2012)

5   McGovern, Patrick E, <u>Ancient Wine: The Search for the Origins of Viniculture</u> (Princeton, NJ: Princeton University Press, 2003) p. 314.

6   Gene M. Heyman, <u>Addiction: A Disorder of Choice</u> (Cambridge, MA: Harvard University Press, 2009) p.4.

7   Gene M. Heyman, <u>Addiction: A Disorder of Choice</u> (Cambridge, MA: Harvard University Press, 2009) p.6.

8   Gene M. Heyman, <u>Addiction: A Disorder of Choice</u> (Cambridge, MA: Harvard University Press, 2009) p.6.

9   Gene M. Heyman, <u>Addiction: A Disorder of Choice</u> (Cambridge, MA: Harvard University Press, 2009) p.7.

10 Gene M. Heyman, <u>Addiction: A Disorder of Choice</u> (Cambridge, MA: Harvard University Press, 2009) p.8.

11 Gene M. Heyman, <u>Addiction: A Disorder of Choice</u> (Cambridge, MA: Harvard University Press, 2009) p.9.

12 Gene M. Heyman, <u>Addiction: A Disorder of Choice</u> (Cambridge, MA: Harvard University Press, 2009) p.18.

13 Gerald G. May, MD, <u>Addiction & Grace</u> (New York, NY: HarperCollins Publishers, 1988) p.43.

14 Harold C. Urschell, III, MD, <u>Healing the Addicted Brain</u> (Naperville, IL: Sourcebooks, Inc, 2009) p.19.

15 AA Grapevine, Inc. <u>http://www.aa.org</u> (July 5, 2012).

16 Lance Dodes, MD, <u>The Heart of Addiction</u> (New York, NY: Harpercollins Publishers, 2002) p.9.

17 Stanton Peele, <u>Diseasing of America</u> (San Francisco, CA: Jossey-Bass Publishers,

1995) p.57.

18 Harold C. Urschell, III, MD, <u>Healing the Addicted Brain</u> (Naperville, IL: Sourcebooks, Inc, 2009) p.7.

19 Harold C. Urschell, III, MD, <u>Healing the Addicted Brain</u> (Naperville, IL: Sourcebooks, Inc, 2009) p.5.

20 Jeffrey A.Schaler, PhD, <u>Addiction is a Choice</u> (Peru, IL: Carus Publishing Company, 2000) p.44.

21 William L.Playfair, MD, <u>The Useful Lie</u> (Wheaton, IL: Crossway Books, 1991) p.58.

22 William L.Playfair, MD, <u>The Useful Lie</u> (Wheaton, IL: Crossway Books, 1991) p.74.

23 Stanton Peele, <u>Diseasing of America</u> (San Francisco, CA: Jossey-Bass Publishers, 1995) p.5.

24 Stanton Peele, <u>Diseasing of America</u> (San Francisco, CA: Jossey-Bass Publishers, 1995) p.5.

25 Stanton Peele, <u>Diseasing of America</u> (San Francisco, CA: Jossey-Bass Publishers, 1995) p.6.

26 Stanton Peele, <u>Diseasing of America</u> (San Francisco, CA: Jossey-Bass Publishers, 1995) p.6.

27 Jeffrey A.Schaler, PhD, <u>Addiction is a Choice</u> (Peru, IL: Carus Publishing Company, 2000) p.16.

28 Gene M. Heyman, <u>Addiction: A Disorder of Choice</u> (Cambridge, MA: Harvard University Press, 2009) p.41-42.

29 Lance Dodes, MD, <u>The Heart of Addiction</u> (New York, NY: Harpercollins Publishers, 2002) p.72.

30 Lance Dodes, MD, <u>The Heart of Addiction</u> (New York, NY: Harpercollins Publishers, 2002) p.81.

31 Lance Dodes, MD, <u>The Heart of Addiction</u> (New York, NY: Harpercollins Publishers, 2002) p.84.

32 Lance Dodes, MD, <u>The Heart of Addiction</u> (New York, NY: Harpercollins Publishers, 2002) p.85.

33 Lance Dodes, MD, <u>The Heart of Addiction</u> (New York, NY: Harpercollins Publishers, 2002) p.86.

34 Gene M. Heyman, <u>Addiction: A Disorder of Choice</u> (Cambridge, MA: Harvard University Press, 2009) p.93.

35 Gene M. Heyman, <u>Addiction: A Disorder of Choice</u> (Cambridge, MA: Harvard University Press, 2009) p.67.

36 Gene M. Heyman, <u>Addiction: A Disorder of Choice</u> (Cambridge, MA: Harvard University Press, 2009) p.152.

37 Gene M. Heyman, <u>Addiction: A Disorder of Choice</u> (Cambridge, MA: Harvard University Press, 2009) p.77.

[38] Gene M. Heyman, Addiction: A Disorder of Choice (Cambridge, MA: Harvard University Press, 2009) p.76.

[39] Lance Dodes, MD, The Heart of Addiction (New York, NY: Harpercollins Publishers, 2002) p.73.

[40] Stanton Peele, Diseasing of America (San Francisco, CA: Jossey-Bass Publishers, 1995) p.26.

[41] Stanton Peele, Diseasing of America (San Francisco, CA: Jossey-Bass Publishers, 1995) p.79.

[42] Abraham J. Twerski, MD, Addictive Thinking (Center City, MN: Hazelden, 1990) p.69.

[43] Stanton Peele, Diseasing of America (San Francisco, CA: Jossey-Bass Publishers, 1995) p.170.

[44] Jeffrey A.Schaler, PhD, Addiction is a Choice (Peru, IL: Carus Publishing Company, 2000) p.37.

[45] Gene M. Heyman, Addiction: A Disorder of Choice (Cambridge, MA: Harvard University Press, 2009) p.99.

[46] Gene M. Heyman, Addiction: A Disorder of Choice (Cambridge, MA: Harvard University Press, 2009) p.173.

[47] Gerald G. May, MD, Addiction & Grace (New York, NY: HarperCollins Publishers, 1988) p.18.

[48] Stanton Peele, Diseasing of America (San Francisco, CA: Jossey-Bass Publishers, 1995) p.59.

[49] Jeffrey A.Schaler, PhD, Addiction is a Choice (Peru, IL: Carus Publishing Company, 2000) p.xiv.

[50] Lance Dodes, MD, The Heart of Addiction (New York, NY: Harpercollins Publishers, 2002) p.139.

[51] Gene M. Heyman, Addiction: A Disorder of Choice (Cambridge, MA: Harvard University Press, 2009) p.171.

[52] Lance Dodes, MD, The Heart of Addiction (New York, NY: Harpercollins Publishers, 2002) p.119.

[53] Stanton Peele, Diseasing of America (San Francisco, CA: Jossey-Bass Publishers, 1995) p.163, 165.

[54] Stanton Peele, Diseasing of America (San Francisco, CA: Jossey-Bass Publishers, 1995) p.200.

[55] Gene M. Heyman, Addiction: A Disorder of Choice (Cambridge, MA: Harvard University Press, 2009) p.84-85.

[56] Lance Dodes, MD, The Heart of Addiction (New York, NY: Harpercollins Publishers, 2002) p.227.

[57] Lance Dodes, MD, The Heart of Addiction (New York, NY: Harpercollins Publishers, 2002) p.22.

[58] Abraham J. Twerski, MD, Addictive Thinking (Center City, MN: Hazelden,

1990) p.113.

59 Gene M. Heyman, <u>Addiction: A Disorder of Choice</u> (Cambridge, MA: Harvard University Press, 2009) p.166.

60 Gene M. Heyman, <u>Addiction: A Disorder of Choice</u> (Cambridge, MA: Harvard University Press, 2009) p.164.

61 Gene M. Heyman, <u>Addiction: A Disorder of Choice</u> (Cambridge, MA: Harvard University Press, 2009) p.165.

62 Abraham J. Twerski, MD, <u>Addictive Thinking</u> (Center City, MN: Hazelden, 1990) p.71.

63 Gerald G. May, MD, <u>Addiction & Grace</u> (New York, NY: HarperCollins Publishers, 1988) p.20.

64 William L.Playfair, MD, <u>The Useful Lie</u> (Wheaton, IL: Crossway Books, 1991) p.59.

65 "sin." *Merriam-Webster.com.* Merriam-Webster, 2012. (July 24, 2012)

66 "paraptoma." <u>The Strongest NIV Exhaustive Concordance</u> (Grand Rapids, MI: Zondervan, 1999) p.1580.

67 Assman, Jan, <u>The Search for God in Ancient Egypt</u> (Ithaca, NY: Cornell University Press., 2001) p1-5.

68 Gerald G. May, MD, <u>Addiction & Grace</u> (New York, NY: HarperCollins Publishers, 1988) p.13.

69 Gerald G. May, MD, <u>Addiction & Grace</u> (New York, NY: HarperCollins Publishers, 1988) p.94.

70 Lee Strobel, <u>The Case for Christ</u> (Grand Rapids, MI: Zondervan, 1998) p.65.

71 Flavius Josephus, <u>Antiquities of the Jews</u> Text from Book 18: Chapter 3, 3.

72 Lee Strobel, <u>The Case for Christ</u> (Grand Rapids, MI: Zondervan, 1998) p.183.

73 Lee Strobel, <u>The Case for Christ</u> (Grand Rapids, MI: Zondervan, 1998) p.265.

74 Gerald G. May, MD, <u>Addiction & Grace</u> (New York, NY: HarperCollins Publishers, 1988) p.115.

75 "repentance." <u>Smith's Bible Dictionary</u> (Uhrichsville, OH: Barbour Publishing) p.260.

76 Francis Chan, <u>Forgotten God</u> (Colorado Springs, CO: David C. Cooke, 2009) p.124.

77 Gerald G. May, MD, <u>Addiction & Grace</u> (New York, NY: HarperCollins Publishers, 1988) p.98.

78 "gennao." <u>The Strongest NIV Exhaustive Concordance</u> (Grand Rapids, MI: Zondervan, 1999) p.1537.

79 Billy Graham, <u>The Holy Spirit</u> (Nashville, TN: Thomas Nelson, 1978) p.113.

80 "parakletos." <u>The Strongest NIV Exhaustive Concordance</u> (Grand Rapids, MI: Zondervan, 1999) p.1580.

81 Billy Graham, <u>The Holy Spirit</u> (Nashville, TN: Thomas Nelson, 1978) p.91.

82 Billy Graham, <u>The Holy Spirit</u> (Nashville, TN: Thomas Nelson, 1978) p.294.

[83] Billy Graham, <u>The Holy Spirit</u> (Nashville, TN: Thomas Nelson, 1978) p.115.

[84] "enkrateia." <u>The Strongest NIV Exhaustive Concordance</u> (Grand Rapids, MI: Zondervan, 1999) p.1543.

[85] Priscilla Shirer, <u>Is That You, God?</u> (Nashville, TN: Lifeway Press, 2009) p.9.

[86] Francis Chan, <u>Forgotten God</u> (Colorado Springs, CO: David C. Cooke, 2009) p.50.

[87] Priscilla Shirer, <u>Is That You, God?</u> (Nashville, TN: Lifeway Press, 2009) p.44.

[88] Billy Graham, <u>The Holy Spirit</u> (Nashville, TN: Thomas Nelson, 1978) p.98.

[89] YouGov.com Survey, "Exorcism and the Devil" September 12, 2013.

[90] "Satanas." <u>The Strongest NIV Exhaustive Concordance</u> (Grand Rapids, MI: Zondervan, 1999) p.1590.

[91] C.S. Lewis, <u>The Screwtape Letters</u> (San Francisco, CA: HarperCollins, 1942) p.32.

[92] Chip Ingram, <u>The Invisible War</u> (Ada, MI: Baker Books, 2007) p.47.

[93] "charis." <u>The Strongest NIV Exhaustive Concordance</u> (Grand Rapids, MI: Zondervan, 1999) p.1602.

[94] "soteria." <u>The Strongest NIV Exhaustive Concordance</u> (Grand Rapids, MI: Zondervan, 1999) p.1596.

[95] "exomologeo." <u>The Strongest NIV Exhaustive Concordance</u> (Grand Rapids, MI: Zondervan, 1999) p.1550.

[96] Gerald G. May, MD, <u>Addiction & Grace</u> (New York, NY: HarperCollins Publishers, 1988) p.6-7.

[97] Gerald G. May, MD, <u>Addiction & Grace</u> (New York, NY: HarperCollins Publishers, 1988) p.153.

[98] Harold C. Urschell, III, MD, <u>Healing the Addicted Brain</u> (Naperville, IL: Sourcebooks, Inc, 2009) p.50.

[99] Harold C. Urschell, III, MD, <u>Healing the Addicted Brain</u> (Naperville, IL: Sourcebooks, Inc, 2009) p.52.

[100] Gene M. Heyman, <u>Addiction: A Disorder of Choice</u> (Cambridge, MA: Harvard University Press, 2009) p.110.

[101] Harold C. Urschell, III, MD, <u>Healing the Addicted Brain</u> (Naperville, IL: Sourcebooks, Inc, 2009) p.60.

[102] "peirasmos." <u>The Strongest NIV Exhaustive Concordance</u> (Grand Rapids, MI: Zondervan, 1999) p.1582.

[103] Wade J. Carey, <u>A Walk Through the Mall</u> (Bloomington, IN: Crossbooks, 2011) p.198.

[104] C.S. Lewis, <u>The Great Divorce</u> (San Francisco, CA: HarperCollins, 1946) p.75.

Printed in the United States
By Bookmasters